*John Metcalf*

Twayne's World Authors Series
**Canadian Literature**

Robert Lecker, Editor
*McGill University*

TWAS 771

JOHN METCALF
(1938–      )
*Photograph by Sam Tata*

# *John Metcalf*

## By Barry Cameron

*University of New Brunswick*

Twayne Publishers

*A Division of G.K. Hall & Co. • Boston*

*John Metcalf*

Barry Cameron

Copyediting supervised by Lewis DeSimone
Book production by Elizabeth Todesco
Book design by Barbara Anderson

Typeset in 11 pt. Garamond
by Modern Graphics, Inc., Weymouth, Massachusetts

Printed on permanent/durable acid-free paper
and bound in the United States of America

**Library of Congress Cataloging-in-Publication Data**

Cameron, Barry.
  John Metcalf.

  (Twayne's world authors series. Canadian literature)
  Bibliography: p. 138
  Includes index.
  1. Metcalf, John, 1938–      —Criticism and
interpretation.   I. Title.   II. Series.
PR9199.3.M45Z6   1986        813'.54         86-11979
ISBN 0-8057-6622-7

# Contents

# About the Author

Barry Cameron is a professor of English at the University of New Brunswick, where he teaches critical theory and Canadian and Renaissance literature. He has published numerous reviews and articles on a wide range of contemporary Canadian writers in addition to articles and reviews on contemporary American poetry and on Chaucer, Donne, and Shakespeare.

He edited the journal *Studies in Canadian Literature* from 1976 to 1979 and was the book review editor of the *Fiddlehead* from 1976 to 1982. With Michael Dixon, he coedited an important collection of critical essays in 1977 called *Minus Canadian: Penultimate Essays on Literature.*

He wrote the chapter on Canadian critical theory and practice for the *Literary History of Canada,* volume 4 (University of Toronto Press, 1987), and the monograph on Clark Blaise for the ECW Canadian Writers and Their Work series (1985). He is also the editor of a forthcoming volume of Donne's verse epistles in *The Variorum Edition of John Donne's Poetry* (University of Missouri Press).

# Preface

Although he has two well-received novels to his credit, John Metcalf is much better known—and deservedly so—as a master of the short story and the novella. In fact, in the latter his only peer in Canadian writing is Mavis Gallant. Metcalf is also one of the most effective and interesting of the very few comic writers Canada has produced, but the ideological premises and the nature of his techniques in this mode have received little, if any, critical attention. Many of Metcalf's fellow writers, however, have long recognized his craftsmanship—indeed, have acknowledged his work as a standard by which to measure themselves. "He knows the aesthetics of his craft," Kent Thompson has written, "and that, besides making him a very good writer, is very important to a number of us. He is setting a standard; he is an artistic conscience; he is the preventer of shoddy work. And that is very important to the development of the short story in this country, in this language."[1]

My concern in this study is above all to offer a reading of Metcalf's fiction that demonstrates both the skilled and interesting ways he manipulates and transforms the conventions of fiction and his deep and abiding interest in the materiality of language. To effect this aim, I have felt it necessary to consider the impact of structuralist and poststructuralist thought on the practice of literary criticism, particularly because in the field of prose fiction so much critical activity has taken place over the past ten years or so. I have accordingly made occasional use of concepts from what has come to be known as narrative poetics or narratology, explaining what might be for some unfamiliar terms as I go along. I should stress, however, that I have done so only when their use renders more accurate an understanding of the fictional transaction I happen to be discussing than more traditional terms would; in some cases, there are no other terms than the ones I use. For the same reason, I have also used several rhetorical terms from classical rhetoric that, though they have been around for two thousand years or so, might also be unfamiliar to some readers. Again I explain these terms when I feel they must be used. Such terms can be immensely useful to students of literature, for they give us a vocabulary to describe certain effects of discourse that would otherwise remain unarticulated in criticism. Given Metcalf's concerns with the manipulative power and emotional efficacy of fiction, it is an entirely appropriate way to speak of his writing. For he is, perhaps more than any other Canadian writer, a consummate rhetorical strategist.

Barry Cameron

*University of New Brunswick*

# Acknowledgments

An earlier version of chapter 4 appeared in *Studies in Canadian Literature* 2 (1977):17–35, and a portion of chapter 5 appeared in a different format in *Fiddlehead*, no. 114 (Summer 1977):57–63.

Thanks are due to Robert Lecker and Anne Jones for their patience and to John Metcalf for his cooperation and permission to quote from all his work. I am also grateful to ECW Press for permission to quote from *The Lady Who Sold Furniture*.

# Abbreviations

In references to the works of John Metcalf, the following abbreviations have been used. The editions cited may be found in the bibliography.

| | |
|---|---|
| GT | "The Geography of Time: Part One" |
| GT2 | "The Geography of Time: Part Two" |
| NCW | *New Canadian Writing, 1969* |
| LSF | *The Lady Who Sold Furniture* |
| GDS | *Going Down Slow* |
| TMF | *The Teeth of My Father* |
| GG | *Girl in Gingham* |
| PP | *Private Parts: A Memoir* |
| GL | *General Ludd* |
| KAP | *Kicking against the Pricks* |

# Chronology

1938    Born 12 November in Carlisle, Cumberland, England. Spends his childhood in Keighley, Bournemouth, and Beckenham, in the last two of which he attended grammar school.

1957–1961    Attends University of Bristol.

1960    B.A. (II,2). Finals paper: "The Creative Imagination (A Study of the Novels of Joyce Cary)."

1961    Certificate in Education.

1961–1962    Teaches at secondary modern school in Bristol and at Borstal.

1962    Immigrates to Montreal. Teaches at Rosemount High School for two years.

1963    First publication, "Early Morning Rabbits," broadcast on the CBC, for which he won a $100 prize.

1964    "Geography of Time," a two-part sequence of stories, published in *Prism International*.

1964–1965    Teaches at Royal Canadian Air Force Base, Cold Lake, Alberta.

1965    Marries Gale Courey.

1965–1966    Teaches at a Catholic comprehensive school in Bristol, England.

1966    Returns to Canada. First anthologized stories, "A Process of Time" and "The Happiest Days," published in *Modern Canadian Stories*.

1967–1969    Teaches at Ross High School.

1968–1971    Awarded Canada Council Short Term Grants.

1969–1971    Teaches at Loyola College, Montreal.

1969    Five Stories published in *New Canadian Writing, 1969*. "The Estuary" awarded the President's Medal, University of Western Ontario, for the best short story of 1968.

| 1970 | *The Lady Who Sold Furniture.* Becomes a Canadian citizen. |
| 1970–1971 | The Montreal Storytellers formed. |
| 1972 | *Going Down Slow.* |
| 1972–1973 | Writer-in-Residence, University of New Brunswick. |
| 1973–1974 | Teaches at Loyola College. |
| 1974 | Wins Canada Council Senior Arts Award. |
| 1974–1975 | Teaches at Vanier College. |
| 1975 | Marries Myrna Teitelbaum. *The Teeth of My Father.* |
| 1975–1976 | Writer-in-Residence, University of Ottawa first term and Loyola College second term. |
| 1976 | Moves to Delta, Ontario. |
| 1978 | Wins Canada Council Senior Arts Award. "Girl in Gingham" and "Private Parts" published together as *Girl in Gingham.* |
| 1980 | *General Ludd.* |
| 1980–1981 | Writer-in-Residence, Concordia University. |
| 1981 | Moves to Ottawa, Ontario. |
| 1982 | *Kicking against the Pricks. Selected Stories.* |

# Chapter One
# Contexts and Poetics

Biographical information can be useful for critics because it tells us about the historical and social circumstances of textual production, an important consideration in understanding fiction as discourse and language as discursive practice. Fiction, because it consists of language, is always a product of a reader in the present moment in the sense that the story does not exist until the reader picks up the text and begins to read, but it is also a product of history because history is inscribed in it at the level of the word or signifier. (For Ferdinand de Saussure, a sign is composed of a signifier [word]—that is, an acoustic image or written shape—and a signified [meaning]—that is, a concept.)[1] All texts, even if they were composed yesterday, are historical texts, and all reading takes place within a practice of reading that is socially determined.

To be concerned with biography in this sense, however, is not, it should be stressed, to explain what transpires in a story in terms of events known to have taken place in the author's life. Such a procedure Metcalf himself would see as "anti-literary,"[2] implying a failure to understand both the essential figural and opaque nature of all language and the nonreferential function of fiction in its fusion and transformation of putative fact and supposed invention. Fictions do not originate with the writer as an originating subject or personality but with other fictions. Most figures in fiction, as Northrop Frye has taught us, descend from earlier figures in fiction, and stories lead us back, as Peter Brooks says, not so much to events as to other stories, "to man as a structure of the fictions he tells about himself."[3] In fact, nothing can be intelligibly said to be prior to language or to originate it. This is not to deny the existence of nonlinguistic phenomena, but it is to say, with Ludwig Wittgenstein, the famous philosopher of language, that verbal activity cannot be better understood or authenticated by referring to nonverbal activities or conditions prior to or contiguous with it.[4]

John Wesley Metcalf was born in Carlisle, Cumberland, in northern England, on 12 November 1938, his father a Methodist minister

whose family, he is proud to say, had farmed in Cumberland for
over three centuries, and his mother a former school teacher.[5] Because his father's profession required frequent transfers, Metcalf spent
his childhood in Keighley, Yorkshire, then the resort city of Bournemouth on the south coast of England, and, finally, in Beckenham,
Kent, a commuter suburb of London. Just before he went to university, however, his father was transferred to Leicester. Listening
often to his father's sermons, as well as to the radio, early in his
life conditioned his awareness of the importance of speech in fiction.
He also spent part of the war years and several subsequent holidays
on his uncle's farm in Cumberland, which affected him lastingly as
"a very real sort of Eden."[6]

He preferred fishing, snake-hunting, and bird-watching to school,
but he also did not care much for school because his older brother
Michael—now a distinguished medieval scholar and lecturer at both
Cambridge and Oxford (at the latter of which he is a Keeper at the
Ashmolean Museum)—had preceded him with such success that
invidious comparisons were sometimes made. Although he and his
brother are now reconciled and he admires Michael a great deal,
there was much hostility between them when they were younger.
He attended grammar school in Bournemouth and Beckenham and
expected to become a boxer when he left school. But because he
had done so well on the English section of the O-level examinations,
for which he had prepared, he says, only to please his parents, the
headmaster of Beckenham, a Mr. White, insisted that he prepare
for A-level examinations, which were necessary for university entrance. Mr. White himself tutored Metcalf in Latin, placing great
demands upon him. But it was this experience of close textual study
together with voluminous reading in the sixth form that Metcalf
credits with teaching him how to read and write. "Words and ideas,"
he says, "were suddenly so real."[7]

Later, having been refused by Cambridge, Metcalf went to the
University of Bristol in 1957 on a scholarship. He read English and
theology under such well-known instuctors as L. C. Knights and
Basil Cottle, but he says, perhaps facetiously, that he was more
concerned with "friendships, sex, drink, rock-climbing, travel in
Europe, and being generally disreputable."[8] An insatiable reader
from childhood, however, he continued to read widely and preco-
ciously on his own, but especially in modern literature, which was
apparently frowned upon at the university, though Metcalf's finals

paper, "The Creative Imagination," was a study of Joyce Cary's novels. His intense interest in Hemingway, another modern, led to an interest in bull-fighting and, twice, to Pamplona for the fiesta where he had a chance meeting with Hemingway himself. Like Hemingway's, Metcalf's dialogue eschews explanatory adverbs and adverbial phrases, the stage directions that frequently accompany dialogue in fiction; and, like Hemingway, Metcalf never uses what might be called disguised definitions as a method of characterization (for example, "her intelligent eyes"). During university vacations he either traveled or worked: once in a Leicester bakery, once as an agricultural worker on the island of Jersey, but most of the time in restaurants.

He earned a B. A. (II,2) in 1960 and a Certificate in Education in 1961, and he then taught at a secondary modern school in Bristol for a year, followed by a temporary position at Borstal, the boys' reformatory, from which, however, he was fired because "he allowed an entire cricket team to escape."[9] While he was at Borstal, Metcalf met James Gaite, now an Australian educational psychologist and university administrator, who persuaded Metcalf to join him in applying to the Protestant School Board of Greater Montreal. They arrived in Canada in the summer of 1962, and Metcalf began work at Rosemount High School teaching English, World History, and, to his chagrin, Canadian history.

It was not long after his arrival in Canada that Metcalf launched his writing career in 1963 by winning a Canadian Broadcasting Corporation short story competition, to which one of his students had drawn his attention. The winning story, "Early Morning Rabbits," was broadcast on the air and garnered a prize of one hundred dollars. Shortly thereafter, at the prompting of Canadian poet Earle Birney, eight of Metcalf's stories were accepted in *Prism International*, the University of British Columbia-based small magazine, and since then Metcalf has considered himself a professional writer.

Because he wished to write full-time, in order to finance his career he took a teaching position in the fall of 1964 at the isolated Royal Canadian Air Force base in Cold Lake, Alberta, in an attempt to save money. While there, he worked on a novel (later abandoned) and on several stories, one of which, "I've Got It Made," was published in the *Canadian Forum* in 1965; he was beginning to gain confidence in his talent. But that Easter of 1965 he returned to Montreal and to a love affair from which he had partially tried to escape by going to Alberta. In August 1965 he married Gale Courey, a student he had met at Rosemount, and the next day they left for Bristol, England.

Metcalf had hoped to live on the money that he had saved and to spend all his time writing, but by September he was forced to take a job as a teacher again, this time in a Catholic comprehensive school. After his Canadian experience, however, England began persistently to irritate him: "Its class attitudes . . . seemed more rigid than ever. It was inefficient and parochial in its attitudes and made me feel cramped. The school was like a lunatic asylum and the children doomed to an easily foreseeable future which was also mine if I didn't remove myself."[10] His decision to return to Canada in 1966 was, consequently, a much more considered one than his initial decision to come to Canada in 1962.

Once again Metcalf taught in a Montreal high school, but he resigned after one year to take a part-time job to enable him to concentrate on writing at "the famous-notorious Ross High School," a private cram school for dense or emotionally disturbed children. "Predecessors in this post had been," he says, Bryan McCarthy, John Mills, Irving Layton, etc. Any poor bugger without a valid teaching certificate."[11] Metcalf was very happy during his two years there with Harry Ross and his wife but had to mark essays for the Protestant School Board to supplement his income. From 1969 to 1971 he taught at Loyola College (now part of Concordia University) where he worked with Sean Kelly, one of the editors of *National Lampoon,* and during 1971–72 part-time at McGill University.

Metcalf was encouraged in his writing during this period by the Ryerson Press fiction editor at that time, Earle Toppings, and his stories began to appear more frequently in Canadian literary magazines. Two, "The Happiest Days" and "A Process of Time," appeared in book form for the first time in the anthology *Modern Canadian Stories* (1966), and others were featured, along with those of Douglas Spettigue and Jerry Newman, in *New Canadian Writing, 1969.* He was awarded the President's Medal of the University of Western Ontario for "The Estuary," judged the best short story published in Canada in 1968; and, as a further sign of recognition, he received Canada Council grants in 1968, 1969, and 1971. His first book, *The Lady Who Sold Furniture,* consisting of a novella and five stories, appeared in 1970, and his first published novel, *Going*

*Down Slow,* followed two years later. In 1970 he became a Canadian citizen.

In the winter of 1970–71 Metcalf and Hugh Hood formed the "Montreal Storytellers Fiction Performance Group"—to use its official name—which also included Clark Blaise, Ray Smith, and Ray Fraser, "to promote Canadian prose to as large an audience as possible by bringing the writers into direct contact with students in high schools, colleges and universities."[12] Because neither the media nor the publishing industry itself seemed to be promoting Canadian literature and because of the "paucity of Canadian literature in high schools and university English courses," Metcalf believed that writers themselves would have "to create and educate an audience for Canadian fiction."[13] The group was forced to disband after a few years but not before it had implicitly proven to the Canada Council, a major Canadian governmental agency that subsidizes the arts, through highly entertaining and instructive performances, that both prose and poetry readings should receive financial support.

Although Metcalf's own level of production was not high, by 1972 he had acquired a strong reputation as a craftsman and as a discerning and caring editor. In the academic year 1972–73 he took up his first writer-in-residence appointment at the University of New Brunswick, but the year was not a particularly productive one because he was suffering the distressing effects of the sudden, unexpected disintegration of his marriage, two years after the birth of his daughter Elizabeth in 1969. He returned to Montreal to teach again at Loyola in 1973–74 and part-time the following academic year at the Snowdon campus of Vanier College. The next year, 1975–76, was split between stints first at the University of Ottawa and then at Loyola as writer-in-residence. He taught one creative writing course at Vanier that fall too. He received his first Canada Council Senior Arts grant in 1974 and a second in 1976, and an important collection of stories, *The Teeth of My Father,* was published in 1975, the same year in which he married Myrna Teitelbaum.

The following year, 1976, they moved with Myrna's son to an old fieldstone house outside the village of Delta, Ontario. Metcalf supported himself by editing and performing various literary assignments for a range of publishers and government arts councils, and he continued to write with the support of another Canada Council Senior grant in 1978 and a short-term one in 1980. Two novellas, "Girl in Gingham" and "Private Parts," were published under the collective title *Girl in Gingham* in 1978, and his second novel, *General Ludd,* was published in 1980. He taught creative writing and was the writer-in-residence at Concordia University in 1980–81. In 1980 the Metcalfs became the guardians of two Sino-Vietnamese refugee children, and later in that same year they adopted two orphan children from South India. The need to provide for such an expanded family forced the Metcalfs to move to Ottawa in June 1981.

Metcalf's anxiety about the cultural conditions under which Canadian literature continues to be produced partially motivated his gathering of occasional autobiographical and polemical essays, *Kicking against the Pricks,* published in 1982, but it was a collection also motivated by his determination to promote modern Canadian literature. This is the driving force, too, behind the many anthologies Metcalf has edited, especially of Canadian fiction, for school, college, and university use as well as several trade collections. Among these the most important are those that include commentaries on their own work by the writers anthologized: *Sixteen by Twelve* (1970), *The Narrative Voice* (1972), *Stories Plus* (1979), and *Making It New* (1982).

Another significant anthology that Metcalf has edited is a special issue of the American quarterly, the *Literary Review* (1985), which contains a range of Canadian stories and complementary critical essays—significant because Metcalf is attempting to introduce several talented Canadian writers to an American audience. Metcalf, in fact, has always been concerned to display the work of his deserving fellow writers, a generosity attested to by his coediting of the annual Oberon series *Best Canadian Stories* from 1976 to 1982 and, with Leon Rooke, of the *New Press Anthology* from 1984. His wish to help lesser-known and younger writers is particularly evident in his initiating and editing of the first three books of the Oberon *Impressions* series, each of which featured three new writers. Were it not for what he sees as the necessity for such editorial work, perhaps his own textual production would be even greater. As he said in an interview with Geoff Hancock, "we're all part of a tradition and if we don't show responsibility to the tradition and extend ourselves for younger writers—even if it's a pain in the ass and takes time away from what we *want* to be doing—then the whole damn thing's going to collapse. I'm not being consciously *nice*. It's a job that has to be done."[14]

It might be fitting to conclude this partial contextualizing of Metcalf's fiction with a comment by a German professor of Canadian literature, Reingard M. Nischik, because it perhaps represents a more detached and accurate statement of Metcalf's place in the literary history of Canada than many—especially those whom he has irritated through his polemical writing—in Canada itself at first blush might be willing to grant:

Metcalf's contribution to the development of the Canadian short story has . . . been manifest and manifold: he has provided new publication forums for writers; he has acted as talent scout; he has helped put the Canadian short story in an international context, freeing it from parochial boundaries; he has guided the attention more to the writing as writing, trying to lead away from the Canadian predilection of regarding writing as, in the last resort, sociological documents; he has contributed to making the Canadian short story better known, also in Canadian schools and universities; he has helped foreground the best writers of short fiction in Canada; last but not least, he is a fine writer of short fiction himself. [15]

## Poetics

For Metcalf, the reality of fiction is an immersion into the ineluctable material conditions of language, into its graphic and phonetic properties: "Stories are a complex totality of feeling and meaning and can only be experienced by immersing oneself in the world they create; this 'immersing' can only be achieved by giving oneself to the *process* of the story, to the story as verbal performance, to its rhetoric, for the story's world lives only in language." [16] No text of narrative fiction, as Gérard Genette has argued, can show or imitate the action it conveys since all such texts are made of language and since language signifies without imitating. [17] Everything, in other words, is "telling" in prose fiction, and since language can only imitate language, all that a story can do is create an illusion, an effect, a semblance of mimesis.

How important the graphic is to Metcalf is suggested in his remarks about writing as a manual activity, what Roland Barthes calls "scription": "It's the actual shaping with a pen and ink of the shapes of the letters on the page that produces the rhythms and the feel of the sentence and the shape of the words." [18] The phonetic qualities of language, as we shall see, are paramount to Metcalf too, but for the moment simply consider his comment about the "traces" of other words (and therefore other meanings in the invented word *tramplings* in "Gentle as Flowers Make the Stones": "I wanted the idea of trampling feet and the idea of *weight* that that implies— the idea that these young women are not exactly sylph-like—and I also wanted a faint suggestion of 'little tramps.' "[19]

Stories, then, for Metcalf are linguistic events not so much to be "understood" as "lived through and experienced."[20] Reading is a performative utterance, and experiencing a story refers to everything relevant going on in our heads and nervous systems as we read. It is largely an unreflective process in that we usually do not watch our own minds. In its simplest terms, when we experience a story, we take in all the information or details of the story as we go along, gathering in new details, creating a pattern out of what we have taken in, and anticipating what will happen or be revealed next. When we read on, our expectations are fulfilled, altered, or dis- appointed, and new information is absorbed and new patterns are projected. It is, however, a game as well as work:

When I think about the act of writing, I often think it's like the play of small children on the beach absorbed in building sandcastles and towns with roads and tunnels all decorated with flags made from popsicle sticks and bits of cigarette packets.
And then the wonderful application of water.
Writing stories has something about it of that tranced pleasure, and I'm convinced that if readers are to share fully in the delight of writing they must be prepared to play *with* writers. . . .[21]

Because of Metcalf's view of story as game, as play, the story insists on itself as production and the signifier as material image takes precedence over the signified as it must for any writer concerned about the material properties of language:

Stories are not puzzles to be solved. Nor do they convey simply moral messages. They are not sermons; they are not propaganda for *any* cause. Their primary purpose, I must insist, is emotional. But that emotional impact will not be felt until the reader has responded with great skill and knowledge to all the nuances of a highly complex performance. *Reading a story is a purely literary activity.*
The reader's final emotional response, however, is *not* literary but it can only be felt by someone with a refined knowledge of and honed skill in the rules of the game. There is a paradox here. . . . genuine *depth* of

emotional response can only be achieved by those willing and able to immerse themselves in amazing artificiality—in language, in literary device, in rhetoric. The 'real,' in other words, is only available to us through an embrace of the unreal and artificial.[22]

It is the words of the story that *produce* the experience, the emotion, not an experience that has produced the words, even as story does not precede text but is constructed through the experience of the text; and in such an experience the reader, playing with the writer, is positioned as the subject of the enunciation (the participant of the speech event, the speaking subject, the producer of meaning) producing the enounced (the narrated event, what is uttered, what is stated). To allow the word to take precedence over the concept, however, does not mean that meaning is unconstrained for Metcalf: "I certainly hope I *don't* use words for their own sake. I only use words that seem to me entirely appropriate with the context and that produce the rhetorical effect I wish to achieve."[23]

Like Vladimir Nabokov and William Carlos Williams, Metcalf knows that literature is not a pattern of ideas but a pattern of images, and, like T. S. Eliot, he knows that good writing is not self-expression but "an invisible iron control of material" that provokes and manipulates emotions in others, emotions from which attitudes and ideas—that is, meaning—might grow: "Good writers aren't usually concerned with expressing 'messages' or with *expressing their feelings.* They're concerned with *causing other people to feel and see.* They're concerned, often quite coldly, with *manipulating* your feelings."[24] What causes people to feel and see, without their necessarily being aware of it, is their response to the texture and rhetoric of the language, for the "realness" of the fictional is offered to us by the texture of the story's language.

Texture, the way in which language is used, "means roughness, smoothness, thickness, delicacy, the 'feel' of the way words are used . . . much the same as a painter means by 'brushwork'—the way paint is applied."[25] Texture obviously draws attention to the materiality of language, and for Metcalf the language of a short story or novella is closer to poetry than it is to other forms of prose discourse, for poetry makes special use of the word or signifier in patterns of repetition and condensation. To avoid the assumption that story precedes discourse, however, we should think of condensation or compression specifically as an effect of the text. Relative to other discourses, poetry thus "foregrounds" the signifier and, through repetition of the signifier, signals that it is to be read as fictional discourse. (Any item in discourse that attracts attention to itself for what is *is*, rather than acting merely as a vehicle of information, may be considered "foregrounded.") Ellipsis and metonymy are characteristics that poetry and good short stories also share; and the concision, density, and complexity of a good short story require the same intensity of reading that poetry requires.[26] Like a good poem, too, a good short story is intense in its emotional effect.

Metcalf's concern with what he calls the *"new verse forms"* of the short story—"imagery, sound, weight, alliteration, assonance," "hints of rhyme and near repetitions," accentual stress in sentences, and the ways in which the play between speech and silence[27] is the oral equivalent of text and white space in poetry—certainly subverts the hegemony of theme, plot, and character in fiction; but Metcalf is still powerfully committed to the representational, to story. (Story, as distinct from text or discourse, refers to the events and situations evoked by a narrative text in their chronological order despite whatever temporal arrangement they may have in the plot as it is dispersed in discourse; it is the story we construct as we read.) Despite the significant metafictional dimensions of such stories as "The Teeth of My Father," "Private Parts," and "The Eastmill Reception Centre" and his awareness of the materiality of language, Metcalf is no outright admirer of postmodernism. "Although my primary loyalties are to style," he says, "I like the artifice and rhetoric to connect me to a real world, actual or imagined."[28]

Like his favorite writer, Evelyn Waugh, Metcalf prefers writers whose technical skill and control are highly developed and whose individual and innovative effects are obtained by a subtle modification rather than a radical readjustment of traditional forms. In Waugh, as well as Kingsley Amis and P. G Wodehouse, two other writers Metcalf admires immensely, it is the balance and elegance of language (timing, pacing, precision, crispness) as well as the comic and the humorous, the wit, that Metcalf savors. He learned much from Waugh, including the cinematic crosscutting and ironic juxtaposition of Waugh's early novels, and, as we shall see when we examine *General Ludd,* Metcalf shares Waugh's elitist and antidemocratic tendencies.

Metcalf, like Waugh, also regards "writing not as an investigation of character but as an exercise in the use of language."[29] Indeed, as he says, "the whole idea of character approached by 'psychology' strikes me more and more as silly, a delusion. The idea of a 'round' character à la Forster is essentially a silly idea. You can't write a 'round' character because you can never *understand* a person fully. All you can do is observe action and listen."[30] "*All* characters in fiction," he says elsewhere, "are artificial constructions; 'round' characters are merely constructed *in a different way* from 'flat' characters. They are no more 'real' . . . often less so."[31] Consequently, like Waugh, Metcalf finds himself attracted to caricature, a type of flat characterization which stresses a single or dominant personality trait with a few secondary ones. Caricatures may be every bit as interesting psychologically as so-called round characters. They may be either highly individualized or stereotyped, and even when they are static rather than developing characters, they may be highly complex. For Metcalf, caricature is a way to create character quickly and vividly: a "quick sketch, a cartoon almost," but "believable"; "an art of essences, of telling detail seized upon and inflated . . . an exaggeration of the most important features." But because "stories should always have imaginative *density,* literary caricatures are not heavy black strokes on blank paper but heavy lines against a background that *suggests* the complexity and detail of a life."[32] Caricatures are also analogous to Jonsonian characterization by "humor," and both types are no less valid than the so-called psychological study:

> The 'psych' portrait or study is as schematic as a 'humour' and possibly with the same amount of 'scientific' validity. To draw a 'choleric' seems to me as valid as more modern counterparts. A psychological portrait or 'profile' is as much a simplification—a counter, if you like, which 'explains' something or stands for something but doesn't embrace the whole. Can't. I think that if the Elizabethans described someone as happy and elated and then suddenly sad they were as accurate as us describing someone as being manic-depressive. It's just that we feel the *words* 'manic-depressive' somehow more scientific and accurate. But no greater *explanation* has taken place. . . .So what I'm saying is that character is endlessly complex but its essentials can be grasped only by simplification and by what issues in action (and speech).[33]

Of these two, action and speech, the latter is more important. Metcalf knows that all texts are realizable orally, that they can be performed, and consequently of the four basic modes of prose fiction—speech, report (action), description, and comment—Metcalf, like so many modern writers, foregrounds speech. For him, voice is central to fiction, and "dialogue or speech is the fastest and probably the best way of suggesting what a person is like"[34]—even his or her physical appearance—because speech, rather than merely providing information, involves the reader intensely in constructing a character through acts of inference and imagination. Characters are merely nodes in the verbal design of the text until we activate that text, constructing characters as personlike abstractions modeled partly on our conception of people.

Speech, whether in dialogue or as a silent activity of the mind, can indicate character both through its content and through its form, and what one character says about another may characterize not only the one spoken about but also the one who speaks. Indeed, the style of a speech often serves as a means of characterization. The voice, the vocabulary, the rhythms (which in themselves may convey emotions and relationships between characters), sentence patterns—all these may imply the past history, social status, education, and profession of a character, both his social and his individual characteristics.

Besides speech, the other major device of characterization on which Metcalf relies and the source of his major imagistic and metaphoric patterns is the metonymic relationships between the external appearances of a character and character traits and between a character's physical surroundings (room, house, street, city) or human environment (family and social class) and character traits. Details of external appearance may be divided into external features beyond the character's control and those that at least partly depend on him, like clothes. While the first type characterizes through contiguity alone, the second has additional causal overtones and is Metcalf's preference, as we shall see. The relationship of contiguity with physical and social setting is also frequently supplemented by that of causality in Metcalf's fiction: "It's possible to say that *setting is also character*. Consider the house or apartment in which a character lives. The objects in a room, or lack of them, the tidiness or clutter, the view from the window—all these things suggest the character of the occupant. They can suggest habits, income, temperament, eccentricity, normalcy, cheerfulness, gloom, etc. etc."[35]

Because Metcalf wishes to exploit the innate possibility of metonymic relationships between character and setting in all its facets, his most frequent point of view is a limited or controlled third-person point of view. The focalization is internal: the narrative is focused through the consciousness (both the perceptual and psychological) of a character, which some theorists of narrative in such a situation call a focalizer or reflector, but the user of the third person is the narrator. Speech is the most neutral and seemingly less authorial of the four fundamental modes, but even when the voice is most like the focalizer's, as in virtual or imagined speech, indirect dialogue, or indirect free speech, it is ultimately the narrator's. Speech certainly comes closest to pure mimesis, but there is always a narrator in prose fiction behind the speech of any character who is "quoting" the character's speech. Yet Metcalf seldom resorts to the voice of the effaced narrator, a narrative technique in which a portion of the narration and description is given in a language attributable to the character whose focus has been assumed by the narrator, while other parts are in a language that must be attributed to the narrator's own understanding and observations. Rather, the language is, with a few exceptions, always appropriate to the focalizer.

The tightly controlled range and concentration on a single individual makes a centered consciousness particularly suitable for the short story and just right for readers, who are close enough yet distanced from the focal character. As Jerome Beaty observes, "The third person keeps us 'other'—we are outside a bit, even as we identify—and the camera eye can pull back, as it cannot do spatially from the first-person narrator."[36] It is a point of view that provides Metcalf with both control and flexibility, with the opportunity to modulate in and out of his central character's mind, to establish levels of fictional reality, and finally to establish levels of voice. This last endeavor is supplemented by his strategic use of such typographical devices as quotation marks, italics, ellipsis, paragraphing, and the dialectic between speech and silence. Finally, except when irony is operating, the ideology of the narrator-focalizer in Metcalf's fiction is usually authoritative and all other ideologies in the text are evaluated from this higher position. But sometimes, as with the detached traveler in "The Strange Aberration of Mr. Ken Smythe," internal focalization is no more than a textual stance.

# Chapter Two
# Beginnings

Rooted in an essentially tragic vision of life, which suggests that there is only effort and absurdity in this world, Metcalf's fiction is a fusion of the humorous and the somber, the absurd and the pathetic, the realistic and the romantic, the satiric and the sentimental. Satire, however, drifts toward either farce or, more frequently, invective, and sentiment occasionally drifts toward either the abyss of sentimentality or melodrama, for both these impulses are hard to control when the primary function of the fiction is to engender a perlocutionary effect of emotion in the reader. The vehicles for these effects are such thematic and imagistic binary oppositions as the relationship between—with the emphasis and implications varying from story to story—the past and the present, Europe and North America, freedom and structure, chaos and order, the individual and society and its institutions, anarchism and authority, the child and the adult, innocence and experience, the pastoral and the urban, the natural or organic and the mechanistic or technological, fictional-poetic truth and factual-historical truth, fact and invention, art and life, autobiography and the autobiographical, reality and fantasy, naïveté and sophistication, the romantic and the cynical. (Cynicism is the common refuge of most romantic sentimentalists.) As with all binary oppositions, however, if we look closely enough, we see that one of the terms is really in a hierarchical relationship to the other, not in a truly dialectical relationship. For instance, the natural, the pastoral, is clearly a privileged concept in many of the stories in the first two groups we shall examine. As Metcalf says in the commentary that accompanies his stories in *Sixteen by Twelve*, "It is only the natural world which *makes sense*. We are a part of the land and its animals—the quality of our relationship is the touchstone of our state of grace."[1] This idea is developed in more subtle and complex ways in the later fiction, but here it is stated in bold romantic terms.

## Early Stories

Thirteen of Metcalf's fictions from the 1960s and early 1970s, including the novella, *The Lady Who Sold Furniture,* and the novel, *Going Down Slow,* are initiation stories, almost as familiar a mode for beginning short story writers as the bildungsroman, the novel of formation or education, is for budding novelists. But several of Metcalf's early efforts eschew the initiation structure and explore other possibilities in the short story. Though technically conventional, these are all well-crafted pieces exhibiting a modern emphasis on "showing" (which, even when the effect is dramatic and immediate, is really a form of effaced telling)—that is, a stress on the modes of speech and report, a concomitant preference for scene over summary, especially scenic report;[2] and, in the third-person stories, an attendant effacement of the narrator. They are good examples, too, of the essence of the short story, compression and intensity, in which less means more; but they are less deeply textured and less thematically subtle than much of Metcalf's later fiction.

"The Beef Curry," from the two-part sequence of stories somewhat pretentiously called "The Geography of Time," is a brief but intense narrative that focuses on the invasion of a restaurant in a predominantly working-class English town by a vulgar works football team from Baldwin and Allcocks (a name not without obvious analogous and punning significance). The point of view is a fixed, cameralike third-person focus of an unnamed young man, but while it is technically an internal focus in that the locus of focalization is inside the represented events, and not from outside, the voice because it is a cameralike focus is that of the narrator. We are other, as Jerome Beaty says, even as we identify with this anonymous but sensitive reflector—his anonymity distances us too—a sensitivity revealed in the several instances of moral apperception that function, as do several of the descriptive details, as the embedded, normative, ideological comment of an implied author. Consider, for instance, the final paragraph, which in its descriptive details of the appearance of one of the footballers, particularly its adjectives, serves as both a metonymic index of the character of the footballer and, because it expresses the young man's moral repudiation of him, thus also indexes the young man's own character:

When he was opposite the man whom the others called Stan, he stopped. He stared at him. He saw the blazer and the gaudy badge, the red-mottled skin of his neck and the careful hair rising to a greasy wave. And then, hurriedly and blushing, he walked on to the door, and pushing it open, went out into the night. (*GT*, 19)

The final sentence reiterates the young man's sense of hesitancy, helplessness, and defeat, complementing two earlier images of paralysis (*GT*, 17; 18–19). The second of these ends with a significant use of the rhetorical device known as isocolon, a figure that repeats phrases of equal length and usually corresponding structure: "He did not even look up when Stan opened the door and took his place at the table, but continued toying with his teaspoon, turning it over and over in the saucer against the side of the cup, turning it over and over against the side of his cup" (*GT*, 18–19). The isocolonic repetition of "turning . . . turning . . ." suggests frustration and ritualized despair, as does the veiled allusion to Eliot's "The Love Song of J. Alfred Prufrock," in which another man is paralyzed by fear.

Through the anonymous young man's sympathetic identification with Paul the waiter, who has been suffering the insults of the footballers, we learn that the fictional world we have just entered is a postlapsarian world of exile: "He spread his soft hands. 'Always I will be the waiter.' A brief sadness deepened his large eyes and he dropped his shoulders in a resigned gesture. Then, as he always did, he said, 'Here is no good. But in Cyprus. . . .' Once Paul had told the young man of the lemon trees and the square houses white in the sunlight. They lapsed into silence. They had not talked, but they had shown sympathy" (*GT*, 15). In the metaphor, Cyprus in the East, with its "lemon trees and the square houses white in the sunlight," is the Eden from which we have been banished. The melancholy and pessimism here, on the edge of sentimentality, are characteristic of one strain of Metcalf's fiction.

The ending of the story is an example of a convention of modern closure, the way stories end: a brief scenic report, a departure, and the rhetorical use of the conjunction "And" to begin the final sentence, which in itself signals closure through its conventional meaning of rhetorical heightening. The opening of the story is likewise conventional modernism in its in-medias-res beginning with scenic report and speech. These are not weaknesses because they are conventional but effective rhetorical strategies. The same cannot be said for the ostentatious use of Hemingway-like repetitions of connectives or conjunctions for rhetorical effect called polysyndeton in one passage of scenic report and the unwitting foregrounding of the verb *cradled* (which Metcalf will use in "Girl in Gingham" with more subtle effect): "The young man straightened and smoothed the check tablecloth, and cradled the cool, chunky Jacobean tumbler in his hands. His glance took in the familiar patterned wallpaper, bright with chefs and pans, and waiters and pots and Eiffel Towers and pavement tables and flowers and carafes of wine, and settled on the private couple" (*GT*, 15). The title of the story is not particularly effective either, offering neither thematic/imagistic direction nor emblematic focus. Marking the beginning of the text, thus constituting it as a commodity,[3] it is merely the occasion of the young man's visit to the restaurant.

But the speech of Paul and especially of the footballers—its accents, its idiom, its rhythms—is superb, speech here functioning revealingly as an index of class, social and moral values, and ethnic origins as well as a metonymic form of characterization. The dispersal of expository details of time and place are handled well too. Yet the vulgarity motif and fixed cameralike focus of an unnamed reflector is used much more effectively and subtly, as we shall see, in "The Strange Aberration of Mr. Ken Smythe," another typological reenactment of the fall.

"Geography of the House" is another story centered on an anonymous young man. As he performs his ablutions in his washroom looking into the mirror, he undergoes an implied epiphany about biological life and the self. The point of view is third-person center of consciousness with several instances of free indirect speech, and the story begins and ends with a scenic report of the self confronting its image—an instance of the convention of repetition known by the rhetorical term epanalepsis, here technically polyptoton—that is, repetition with a difference. In epanalepsis an element that begins a clause, sentence, paragraph, or larger unit of discourse is repeated at the end; the element may be a verbal one, scenic, psychological, or modal, but whatever form it takes, the repetition creates a sense of a frame and therefore establishes closure: "The young man stood over the wash basin and glanced at his reflection in the mirror. . . . He dried his hands slowly on the towel and turned to leave the bathroom. Then suddenly, he turned again, and peered closely into

the mirror at his image" (*GT,* 35). The ascendance on the style
register here in the last sentence is also a device writers often use
to signal closure. The title of the story is a bit more effective this
time, echoing the title of the sequence of stories in which it appears
and perhaps alluding to both places of the house (bathroom) and
body (heart). There is thus much technical expertise displayed here,
but the trivial theme of self-reflected knowledge and the brevity of
the story make it seem no more than an exercise, a limbering up.

Much more important because their fictional world forms a context of subject matter and theme for Metcalf's two novels are "A
Process of Time" and "The Happiest Days." They are the best stories
in the sequence "The Geography of Time," worthy of being Metcalf's first anthologized stories.[4] They are companion pieces, both
first-person narratives that focus on the psychological disintegration
of teachers within the school system.

"A Process of Time" opens with a conventional in-medias-res
scenic report indicating habitual behavior and fusing description,
indirect discourse, and embedded comment: "Neanderthal Man was,
as usual, hogging the only kettle in the staff-room. He was resting
his paunch on the edge of the sink and baying on about attendance
registers, scraps of paper in the corridors, the ignorance of today's
Youth, and the scurrilous nature of the inscriptions on the walls of
the boys' lavatories. When I saw Peking Man coming to join us, I
abandoned the idea of coffee and went to sit down until the bell
rang" (*GT,* 27). Emphasizing speech as a narrative mode, both
direct and indirect, and indulging in his characterization preference
for caricature and grotesque, Metcalf shows us the gradual surrender—there is a subtle military as well as a paleontological motif
running throughout the story—of one Mr. Adams (the name is not
without allegorical significance, an instance of characterization by
analogy: Adam was the first fallen man). After some virtual speech
and virtual description that caricatures his principal as the Gnome,
we read of Adams's only victory, the "petty" one he wins with Miss
Rita Brown, one of the first in a long line of Metcalfian grotesques.

During the poetry lesson Adams then conducts with his class,
Metcalf nicely intersperses expository details of the setting at the
same time suggesting by their interjection the labored pace of the
class. The figurality of Adams's "hollow" desk is an obvious touch,
not as subtle as the analogical possibilities in the zeugma, "I looked
up at the rows of leaden faces and the drooping flag in the corner,"

which identifies the two objects of the verb (*GT*, 28). (A zeugma is a rhetorical figure in which one verb governs several congruent words or clauses, each in a different way.)

Things begin to droop even more once the Gnome enters the classroom in a surprise inspection, and we witness the embarrassing and "slow process" of the defeat of Adams through the Gnome's— unwarranted in terms of the prevailing moral norms of the story— assault on Tony Bennet, the only student singled out as a positive norm during the poetry lesson. While the assault is taking place, Adams at first pretends to be checking something in his notebook, and then later, he "walked over to the window and pretended to look out" (*GT*, 30). Finally, he completely self-destructs. Another Adam falls:

I was still looking out of the window when the Gnome said, "Mr. Adams! Are you sure you find this boy's work entirely satisfactory? Every other teacher in the school seems to think rather differently from you. Are you positive?"

I heard a strange voice speaking in the tense silence. It said, "Well, as a matter of fact, I don't remember ever seeing his last English homework." (*GT*, 30)

The ending of the story is an instance of epanaleptic closure in which the title of the story is repeated, a repetition effecting the sense of a frame, but Metcalf also makes use of the figure of repetition called *conduplicatio*—that is, repetition of words in succeeding clauses—here to draw attention to the fact that Adams's remarks ironically apply to the erosion, the attrition, of himself and his integrity. They also implicitly suggest that he too will become, if he has not done so already by his capitulation, either Neanderthal or Peking man:

In the staff-room at recess, Peking Man waddled through the kitchen door and came to sit down next to me. He said, "We can't allow them to get away with it, you know."

"What?" I said.

"Words in the lavatories," he said.

"It's a slow process," I said. "A process of attrition."

"I suppose you're right," he said.
"A process of time," I said.

(GT, 30)

Exploring a dialectic between the past and the present, the child and the adult, fantasy and reality, and freedom and discipline, "The Happiest Days" is a much more sophisticated story, in both theme and technique, than "A Process of Time." Its synecdochic structure is much more evocative too: we infer a great deal about the introverted narrator from this momentary glimpse into his defeated life in the classroom on a certain Wednesday, and the use of the present tense suggests not immediacy but that it is an ongoing psychological condition. A retrospective narrative would imply some coming-to-terms, some acceptance. The language of the story is also much more deeply textured than the stories we have examined so far, presaging things to come.

The story begins in-medias-res with a scenic report that immediately suggests in its mathematical and litanic connotations the soul-destroying, regimented quality of the narrator's exterior life. This outward action is then juxtaposed with the teacher's internal condition: his wish to speak understandingly and to be anarchistic, unrestrained, playful, and libidinous:[5]

The report cards are yellow with brown printing. I am filling in the numbers black Pass red Fail; the aggregate and average attendance for the months of September, October, November, and December excluding Public Holidays; Character Traits; Citizenship, Honesty, Cooperation, Practicality and Idealism.

I am secretly looking at the children. They are supposed to be working and are not. Sometimes it is like a trance. The chalk stops in the middle of its loops and squeaks, and I want to say something, but cannot. They would not understand. I want to say, "I know. I understand." I would like to rend the neat divisions of their minds, break the rules, shout "Bum." (GT2, 30)

This desire complements his envy of his students' vital, surging lives: "Like an unwanted child, seeming unconcerned on the borders of the game, I watch them when they play. Twenty years young I ran with you, played the ball, knocked out imaginary teeth, and, as it seems, was happy" (GT2, 30). And so, standing now in the "falling," postlapsarian world "of chalk-dust," he recalls a happy pastoral image of his youth, a flashback, which is followed by another one chronologically subsequent to the first:

In the wood was an old holly tree whose bark was scabbed and peeled like ivory. Some twenty feet above the ground a large branch formed a natural seat, and the glossy leaves made a cage around it, hiding you from view. . . .
  Below the large branch was a thinner one and David always used to Tarzan-drop through the terrifying space to grasp it, swinging until the bouncing stopped. He never actually said anything to me but I knew. Why should I remember that now?
  Years later, after I had been working some two or three years, I went back to the old town, to the wood, to the tree, and everything was still the same. The same tree, the same branches, the same boys though they were different.
  We talked and I did the jump—an easy grasp—a drop of two feet, and I swung there for a moment and dropped to the ground. One of the boys said, "We do that, mister." And I said, "I know," and went away. (*GT*2, 30)

Notice how "terrifying" the space is between the two branches in the earlier scene—a measure of the space between the vitality of youth and the imaginative impoverishment of adulthood, a lament complemented by the other remembered details from his child-hood—about playing marbles, for example.

One of the ways the story moves imagistically is the contrast, interjected in expository sections, between the cactus plants, me-tonymically signifying a sterile environment, a desert, inside his room and the metaphoric "field dotted with white flowers" reported through flashback of the Last Sports Day by the sunshine and white clouds outside (*GT*2, 31). The inside-outside contrast here mirrors in reverse the outside-inside contrast between his external behavior and his inner wishes. The poles of the imagistic contrast are joined by the common detail of sand, and the image of the warm outdoors is identified with the earlier pastoral daytime image of the wood and holly tree, even as the cactus plants are identified with the "nightmare babble of voices" about cars and gardens in the staff room (*GT*2, 31).[6] The activity of the first part of the Sports Day serves as a wished-for sense of communion (contrasting with the nightmare babble) or symposium (suggested by the reference to ancient Greece) with others and as a cultural norm. That sense of oneness is undermined, however, by the ironic but appropriate parallels between the narrator and T. S. Eliot's Prufrock—another fearful, introverted, socially intimidated figure, another of the living dead identified with dead ritual—and by the shattering of the moment by a mob of boys throwing a football, from which Adams flinches away as he always does.

From this remembered scene of the Sports Day, the teacher returns to the litany of the report cards, which spawns a fantasy of the vulgar daydreams of the working-class student whom the narrator really envies the most, Tony Fielding. This is followed shortly after by a dramatic hypotyposis—that is, a description of people and events that exist in imagination only, a fusion of virtual report and virtual description—involving a fantasized confrontation between the narrator and Fielding during which the narrator deliberately provokes the student to attack him. He does not defend himself in this fantasy, however, because he really wishes to be punished, to be let out—notice the emphasis created by isolating "At last" as a sentence fragment—in order to expiate his guilt, one aspect of which is that he is himself an agent of repression and discipline, the very thing from which he wishes to escape:

Fielding is growing angry and confused. I take hold of his tie near the knot. "You'd be better off, Fielding, if you spent less time with that creature who hangs around the school gate for you. Wouldn't you?" I pull sharply on his tie.

He knocks away my hand and glares at me. "Would you, Fielding? You haven't got the guts." I turn away and hear him get up. At last. He pulls me round and his first punch hits me high on the shoulder. I make no defence. He hits me again, this time in the mouth and I feel the numb impact of his knuckles and then the releasing pain. He hits me again and again in the face and stomach and still I stand there for there is no defence. (GT2, 32–33)

The story ends with epanalepsis—technically the figure is polyptoton, repetition with a difference—by repeating a passage that bridges the first virtual report about Fielding with the second, more dramatic one, which, as we have seen before, provides closure but much more significantly indicates the status of the confrontation with Fielding as fantasy and reiterates the psychological themes of fear and discipline. Notice the rearrangement of the sentences—an instance of auxesis (placing clauses in climatic order) as well as polyptoton—implying that the new final sentence, which was in the middle in the first occurrence, traditionally the position of least rhetorical emphasis, is now rhetorically the most important—showing guilt and the fear of reprisal: "The noise of their chatter is irritating and disturbs my work. The noise has risen to a ridiculous level and I must keep them quiet. Soon Mr. Benson in the next room will hammer on the wall and they will talk about me in the staff room again" (*GT*2, 33). The clipped, spare sentences here are appropriate too, especially in contrast to, say, the rhythmic flow of the first virtual report on Tony Fielding.

Metcalf has provided several *amorce* for the teacher's final failure. (The term is Genette's[7] and means a preparation of or a hinting at a future occurrence, a device Metcalf will use again with great skill in "Girl in Gingham" among other stories.) Early in the story, we learn of his "secretly looking at the children" (*GT*2, 29) followed shortly after by the descriptive report: "Like an unwanted child, seeming unconcerned on the borders of the game, I watch them when they play" (*GT*2, 30), another image of an alienated observer on the edge of life. These details are complemented by his flinching away, as he always does, he says, when the football was kicked across his path on the Sports Day and, of course, by the first remark about his fear of being talked about in the staff room again.

The title is an effective control functioning as an ideological norm and suggesting in its plurality both lost days of youth and their only approximation, however impoverished, the last Sports Day. Like Prufrock, a frustrated, divided man, the narrator is haunted not only by a knowledge of the pettiness and triviality of the world, but also by a sense that he once had a vision of life more real and beautiful but that he has descended from that primordial vision into the present sterile existence that now chokes him. The story is an important one in its own terms, but it is also an interesting prelude to Metcalf's similar but even more interesting development of the notion of anarchistic desire, vulgarity, and freedom in "The Eastmill Reception Centre" and "Private Parts."

## Marriage

Three of Metcalf's stories, his weakest, center on ironic relationships between husband and wife: "A Toy Called Peter Dog" and "Consequences" end the sequence "The Geography of Time," and the third story, "One for Cupid," is fortunately buried in the small magazine *Edge*. They are weak stories not only because their subject matter is trite and clichéd, but also because they lack the richness and subtlety of his best stories. They are nevertheless interesting for some of their technical flashes.

"A Toy Called Peter Dog" reveals through a third-person center of consciousness a man's real and ironic relationship to his wife. Prevented from spending the rest of a certain evening with his friends David and Jim, the reflector, Peter, must head for home after a phone call to his wife, this last detail an interesting example of what Roland Barthes calls a nuclei event or Seymour Chatman calls a kernel event.[8] (There are two types of events in narrative: those that advance the action by presenting an alternative—kernels or nuclei, and those that extend, expand, amplify, delay, or maintain the former—catalysts or satellites.) What follows after the phone call is a series of too-telling catalysts that index his fallen attitude toward his wife initiated by his dropping the phone "into its rest with a loud crash" (*GT*2, 39): Walking along "with a tight constricted feeling in his chest" and his left shoe accidentally filled with "icy slush," he takes perverse pleasure in the "discomfort of each sodden step" (*GT*2, 39); when he arrives at his apartment building, he allows "himself the pleasure of letting the heavy door slam behind him as he started up the stairs" (*GT*2, 39), but hoping that he won't have to confront his wife, as he approaches his front door he holds his breath and walks as quietly as he can, opening the door carefully and "making sure that his keys did not jangle" (*GT*2, 39).

This sequence of action is then followed by another set of corroborating reportorial and descriptive details, among which are two blatant similes suggesting guilt and criminality: "The house was all about him. Then, life [*sic*] a thief, he made his way silently to the kitchen. Marjorie called out, 'Is that you, Pete?' He stood in the darkness of the kitchen hoping that the floor would not creak. . . . The room was filled with a harsh glare, like the interrogation room in a prison" (*GT*2, 39). The obvious series of metonymic signifiers that now follow signify the squalidness of domestic life from Peter's point of view: the emblematic—because it is the title of the story—toy rabbit Peter Dog, a "hideous thing" with a "sagging middle"; Marjorie's "ugly pyjamas, buttoned to the throat," that remind "him of a Salvation Army handout"; the array of feminine articles on top of the dressing table, "sad rearguards

against the advance of time"; and, "hanging on the back of the
kitchen door, his wife's old blue dressing gown," "the pile of the
wool on the lapels" of which "was stiff and crusted with milk and
dribble" and "smelled of babies" (*GT*2, 40).This last detail is the
most interesting because it ironically recalls Peter's implicit lament
for the childlike, idyllic (perhaps pre-baby) past of their marriage:

> On the far wall there was a reproduction of an early Picasso. Peter looked
> at the pure strong curve of the woman's back and wondered why it made
> him feel slightly sad. Perhaps it was the beer. Marjorie had a funny little
> mark on her back. Just at the bottom of the ribs on the left. It was half-
> way between a mole and a beauty-spot. He smiled slightly and raised his
> glass ironically to the perfection of the painting. Once, what seemed now
> a long time ago, it had had a name. They had called it Mole." (*GT*2, 38)

There is perhaps an allusion to Kenneth Grahame's *The Wind in
the Willows* here, especially because of the pastoral and childlike
implications in the allusion. The book is an entrance into rivers,
fields, and woods that release us from the requirements of responsible
human life into holiday.[9] But the perfection of the painting implies
the imperfection of the flesh-and-blood Marjorie, and in fact the
details about ribs and the left evoke the traditionally phallocentric
view of the "sinister" Eve of, say, Milton who may be connected
with the bitch goddesses of Hemingway.

Earlier in the story, of course, Peter's friends, David and Jim,
were arguing about Hemingway and refer to two Hemingway stories, "Hills like White Elephants" and "Cat in the Rain," both of
which deal ironically with the victimization of women. In the first,
a story of sterility and despair, at the subtle urging of her lover, a
woman unwillingly commits herself to an abortion, and in the
second some commentators have seen the wife's desire for the kitty
as a symbolic wish for a child. The reference in the discussion to
"the hairy-chest stuff" (*GT*2, 37) associated with Hemingway and
to possible homosexuality reminds us too of the male bonding Peter
is being denied because of his domestic life. The story ends with a
heavy-handed irony, a form of rhetorical heightening that here signals closure: "He went over to the bed and stood looking down at
her. She looked away from him and he bent and opened the top
button of her pyjamas. He sat on the edge of the bed and turned
her head towards him. As he kissed her, he mumbled, 'You *know*
its [*sic*] not fair to hide a beautiful neck like that' " (*GT*2, 40).

This is the best of the three marriage stories. It is certainly better than its sequel, "Consequences," which focuses on the husband's guilt, again in a third-person center of consciousness. Lying in bed, confronted with the "barrier of her back," "the accusation of her back," he realizes that "when you were grown up you could no longer say 'Pax' and halt the game. You could no longer say 'I'm sorry.' Consequences was a ritual game. You could—no longer—say 'I'm sorry' " (*GT*2, 42). And so the story slides to an obvious Freudian dream of childhood innocence in which, though innocent, he is repudiated, rejected by his mother, and we are meant to draw the obvious parallels to his present situation (*GT*2, 43). The story ends with the convention of turning away; even as his mother did, his wife now rejects him: "He struggled out of the blackness and the echoing scream, and found that he had moved across the bed closer to his wife. He lay quietly in the darkness and listened to the jerky rhythm of the clock. Her breathing was soft and regular. Carefully he put his face against her shoulder, but she mumbled in her sleep and shrugged away" (*GT*2, 43).

"One for Cupid" raises an interesting problem if one were to think of the writer not as an inferred author, an effect of fictional discourse that might vary from story to story, but as a point of origin and unity. Critics frequently attempt, for example, to make an individual writer the stylistic source of the homogeneity of a gathering of texts; the problem is that this treatment of the writer as a single, unified individual does not allow for the possibility of stylistic heterogeneity. Thus Douglas Rollins finds "One for Cupid" an aberration of Metcalf's style, a "strangely anomalous" story.[10] It is certainly different: a stylistically clichéd Americanesque story— almost like a 1950s "small film"[11] of, say, a Paddy Chayefsky teleplay in its dramatization of a clichéd American lower middle-class domestic confrontation between a middle-aged Helen and Harry. Speech is the dominant mode, thus mitigating the sense of mediation between story and reader. After meaninglessly sniping at each other for over four pages, Harry predictably has a flashback about his one-time triumph playing cards when he "walked like a king." He is a loser now, of course, and so the story ends ludicrously with Harry reduced to the level of a child sucking his wife's "sagging white breast" for comfort and security.

Because it concerns the debilitating effects of failed marriages, it is convenient to treat a much later story, "Playground," in the context of these early stories that center on marriage. The story was commissioned by the CBC: eighteen pages demanded and eighteen pages delivered, not an easy feat. In retrospect, however, Metcalf sees the story as "shockingly bad"—on what grounds, he does not elaborate.[12] Its subject matter is certainly the stuff of soap opera, trite and clichéd: Peter Lawson, psychologist and recently divorced father, takes his four-year-old visiting daughter to a local park every day to help pass the time. There he encounters an ultimately willing young mother, ironically named Felicity, who is fundamentally unhappy with her marriage. Through a few strategically placed *amorce* (he observes the amplitude of her breasts when he first sees her and can't help noticing the elastic of her panties through her jeans), we know that they are going to get together sexually. Sure enough, one noon hour, while the kids are mucking about in her conveniently located house close to the park, they go to it in a locked bedroom. But this is not the only problem with the story: the anterior report about his former wife's behavior is "shockingly" melodramatic.[13]

Yet the story is interesting in terms of its use of a third-person center of consciousness and the successfully sustained use of a variety of levels of indirect speech, which foregrounds dialogue whenever it occurs, from summary through indirect discourse and indirect discourse mimetic to some degree to free indirect discourse.[14] Like the other stories in this group, "Playground" is nevertheless not a strong story.

## Collected Stories

"Walking Around the City," the first of the four collected stories treated in this section, is a clear example of Metcalf's Eliotic principle that good stories should elicit emotion—in this case, sadness—in the reader. Writing is neither therapeutic nor self-expressive for Metcalf, for, as he says in an interview conducted in 1975, "what all writers are trying to do is to provoke and manipulate emotions in other people. You can't afford to feel if you are trying to provoke emotions in others because you don't have the necessary detachment and control." He goes on to give an example of this difference between emotion felt and emotion produced by the writer that is highly relevant to the story at hand: "When I teach writing classes, I say to kids, 'Okay, your dog got run over, and you loved your dog. So you come in and you write the thing and you say, "I'm very unhappy today, I'm sad, because my dog got run over." I look at it and say, "Oh, poor kid. His dog got run over," and then I give it back and say, "Now, that for *you* is therapeutic because you've written down how sad you feel. But that's not your job. Your job is to draw pictures of a dog with intestines hanging out, whimpering, and with a last breath licking his master's hand to make *me* feel sad." ' I think that's the essential difference."[15]

The great risk a writer runs with such a poetic, of course, is sentimentality—generating an emotional response in excess of that warranted—no matter how austere the style and understated the reflector's responses might be. Indeed, understatement tends to magnify emotional response, as does Metcalf's use, here and elsewhere, of Waugh-like ironic juxtapositions. The incongruity, the perceived indecorum, of the contiguous details stresses their difference and intensifies the emotional impact resulting from the apperception of that difference. The accumulated effect is that the horror of the indifference of the world to the plight of the wounded dog in this story exceeds the horror of the dog's condition.

The title of the story ironically belies our expectations: this is no pleasant scenic tour of the city's charming place attractions, but a devastating excursion into the mechanistic neon vulgarity and dark moral callousness (the setting at night is a metonymic signifier) of the city. Cityscape is indeed a moral landscape here. The titles of Metcalf's stories seem to be more effective in the collected stories, and they are an important controlling focus in composition: " . . . I can't even begin to write a story unless I have a title—perhaps because in some way the title defines for me what it is I want to attempt to say."[16]

A first-person narrative, the story plunges us immediately into drama:

I heard the engine climbing from the stop sign and saw the headlights boring round the corner, sweeping in to colour the hedge, the lower branches of the tree, the lawn's edge. "Hold her!" I yelled across the road to the boy but at the sound of my voice she lunged forward. I saw the white flash on her chest as she launched herself and then I heard a dull, rolling thud as the car smashed into her. I heard her scream three or four times and then the car was sweeping on up the hill. I ran across to where she lay curled in the gutter. (*NCW*, 21)

The natural (dog) and the mechanistic (car) are obviously in antithesis here, and the story leads us through a series of analogues of this initiating action, each of them a failure of grace, each an exemplary instance of man's indifference and callousness to the natural world, as the narrator futilely attempts to save the dog: the driver of a passing car who says, "You're blocking the road there" (*NCW*, 21); the juxtaposed action in a neighboring house, to which he has taken the wounded animal, of the boy's watching the hockey game on television and the pathetic condition of the dog (*NCW*, 22); the cabdriver who wants "no mess on the seats" (*NCW*, 23) as the narrator takes her to the Vet's Hospital; the absurdity of the situation at the Vet's Hospital itself where he is told to go away and phone back the very person to whom he is speaking; the unaided struggle to get to the SPCA only to find no one there who can help; and, finally, the humiliating absurdity of his confrontation with the police who do not believe that he is carrying her dead body in the bag.

There are two extremely effective instances of metonymic moral signification generated through ironic juxtaposition. The first is the descriptive vulgarity of the cab and the Hot Line Show on the car radio in the cab during which one caller seriously suggests that criminals, like animals, be inhumanly castrated. This is the moral and cultural world we inhabit: "I lit a cigarette and sat watching the patterns of passing light, the maze of headlights and tail lights, the moving blocks of buses. Across the road, a neon sign, in flickering green and yellow, repeatedly spelled out *Pizza Palace*. People sat in their cars on the forecourt eating food from cardboard boxes with plastic utensils. A lady wearing cowboy boots and a short skirt trotted from car to car" (*NCW*, 27–28). The two most stunningly pathetic moments in the story are the dog's death (*NCW*, 27) and the narrator's final searing moment of pain, his wish to atone for her death, to pay bitterly for the world's cruelty to one of nature's own: "I wanted to hold the burden of her body in my arms and walk until the pain seared the muscles in my back and shoulders at every step. I wanted to walk past all the Pizza Parlours, the used-car lots strung with coloured lights, the Kerb Kings, the Dairy Queens, the homes of the Babyburgers, and all the clean glass palaces where faces stared out at the passers-by. I wanted to feel at each plodding step the cold shit rubbing against my body; I wanted to smell with each step the stench of her death" (*NCW*, 29). The

anaphoric repetition of "I wanted" intensifies an already emphatic
rhetorical heightening, which here signals closure.

"Robert, standing" is another story that runs the risk of sentimentality because it is a portrait—the title suggests in one of its
senses a painting, a pose—of a paraplegic on one morning of his
life that synecdochically reveals the depth of loneliness in his life.
The point of view is an internal third-person center of consciousness
with significant amounts of substitutionary perception: we see what
Robert thinks, sees, and feels only through his consciousness.

The particularity and vividness of the narrative details, in which
description and report are thoroughly fused, as Robert goes·about
his morning routine of washing, dressing, and getting organized
ring with authenticity. The external-internal, visual-thought juxtaposition of the movement of the drop of water on the tile that
finally drops "down below the edge of the tub and out of sight"
(*NCW*, 32)—a sort of visual emblem of Robert—and what Robert
is thinking is also effective. This external-internal pattern continues,
and through it we learn of Robert's loneliness and implicit sexual
longing. (There may even be a buried sexual pun in the title.) We
wonder, for example, who the "she" is in the following passage—
a friend of Robert's, a sister, a colleague, a lover?—only to discover
two paragraphs later that pathetically she is a waitress who unwittingly offers a glimpse of her flesh: "It was three days now since
he'd been out. But if he went a bit later she wouldn't be so busy.
One-thirty. One-thirty might be better, when the cars had thinned
out. . . . Bring his tray, the edge of the peasant blouse decorated
with blue and pink stitched flowers. Leaning into the carriage, the
blouse falling away, a tiny gold crucifix on a gold chain deep between
her breasts" (*NCW*, 32). We see him rush to greet the mailman
and hear the irony of the mailman's implied satisfaction at being
back on the job after a holiday, "Oh, it gets kind of boring round
the house" (*NCW*, 35)—ironic because it of course applies to Robert's condition.

And so when two young "messengers of the Lord" come calling
(*NCW*, 35), a Miss Adetti and a Miss Stevens of the Church of
Jesus Christ of Latter-day Saints (Mormons), Robert immediately
welcomes them, not because he is interested in the messages but
because he is starved for human company. What he notices are the
physical appearances of the girls, their bodies and clothes, and such
a selection of details immediately foregrounds them and Robert's

interest. The most telling of these substitutionary perceptions concerns Miss Stevens: "Robert saw with sudden interest that her baggy blouse concealed absolutely enormous breasts" (*NCW*, 38).

There is no real communication going on here. All the remarks of the girls are automatic. The story ends with their departure and Robert's final remark revealing the implicit anguish of his reduced condition and epanaleptically echoing the title of the story:

"Hey! You!"
Two startled faces turned to stare at him. His body bent forward from the chair.
"If I was standing up," he bellowed, "I'd be six foot three."(*NCW*, 40)

There is a sense in which Robert is "standing up" for himself here by speaking up, and the departure, epanalepsis, and rhetorical heightening are effective conventions for ending the story.

The title of the story "Dandelions" is also a nuanced one. The jam jar of dandelions envisioned through a daydream window by one George Kenway, a middle-aged bookseller, is a point of emblematic focus for his wished-for but lost life:

He saw a small boy standing in a familiar room looking towards the window. The boy was himself. He was standing alone in the big stone-flagged kitchen. He could feel the coolness of the stone through his stocking-feet. Behind him, on the mantelpiece, the black clock was ticking.
On the red-tiled window sill stood a jam jar full of dandelions. The window burned. Between the lace curtains, sunlight, sunshine glittering off the silver tap, gleaming in the white sink, glowing on the crowded yellow heads. (*LSF*, 147)

The point of view is internal, a third-person center of consciousness with some free indirect discourse and dialogue, an abundance of substitutionary perception, and one important instance of virtual description onto which is tagged a couple of lines of virtual speech: George's imagined vision of his store as a real antiquarian bookstore.

In contrast to his lost, buried life is the cramped, mundane routine of his present existence metonymically signified in his physical ailments and the accumulated effect of such items as the venetian blind with its buckled slat; his sandwiches "wrapped in grease-proof paper and secured with an elastic band" (*LSF*, 145); the gray cardigan with mother of pearl buttons his wife, Mary, has knitted him; the pencil in his hand doodling "over the yellow pad drawing tiny, interlocking circles in endless repetitions" (*LSF,* 144); his pocket watch with the glass "scratched and yellowed" that belonged to his father and for which "Mary had made a shammy-leather pocket for it in the waistband of his trousers" (*LSF,* 144); his fountain pen, "a gift from Mary eleven years ago" (*LSF,* 146); the green blotter; the Castaneda box; the tin box; Roy's bike; and the hedge.

The host of routine activities that he performs reinforce the familiar mundaneness of his life—the way he checks the door before he leaves, for example, or the way he gets "automatically to his feet just before his stop" (*LSF,* 148)—but that he leaves for home early, vaguely disturbed, suggests the buried conflict in his life. How buried it really is is suggested by the illusory effects of his clipping the hedge toward the end of the story and the resulting cerebral numbness indicated by his failure to recollect his lost dream immediately after, at the very end of the story, closure being signaled by the use of a "but" clause: "There was a light, sharp scent in the air, a faintly acid smell. The smell of sap and bruised privet leaves. It seemed to move a memory in him . . . a recollection . . . but he could not remember what it was" (*LSF,* 150). The smell of sap and bruised privet leaves, an image from the natural world, is identified with the dandelions, and the failure in memory complements the other, earlier instances of failed memory: "He had forgotten to empty the tin cash-box" (*LSF,* 148); "He had forgotten the oil for the clippers" (*LSF,* 149).

"The Estuary," for which Metcalf won the University of Western Ontario President's Medal for the best single story of 1968, also explores the stultifying mundaneness of date-stamped urban existence: the "sullen gathering of boredom which ripens every few weeks screaming for the lancet" (*NCW,* 54). The story, a first-person narrative in which the narrator also participates, is told by a young assistant librarian who is putatively undergoing psychiatric therapy, and it is a good example of what Seymour Chatman means by a plot of revelation as distinct from a plot of resolution. In the plot of revelation, it is not that events are not "resolved (happily or tragically) but rather that a state of affairs is revealed," and "revelatory plots tend to be strongly character-oriented, concerned with the infinite detailing of existents"[17]—that is, characters and items of setting, the latter of which tend to be metonyms of character. We are concerned in "The Estuary" not with what will happen, as we would be in a "hermeneutic" narrative of resolution, but with the questions: why is the central character tired, why is he undergoing so-called treatment, did he really try to commit suicide and, if so, why? The development of the story leads not to a resolving but to a displaying. And an interesting and ironic display it is as we discover that it is not David who is mad but the world in which he lives—"It is only the natural world that *makes sense*"[18]—and that his walk into the sea is not toward death but life. It is the opposite of suicide, an attempt to break the bonds of the prison of living death in which he exists by seeking the beauty and freedom represented by the porpoises.

The story begins conventionally in-medias-res but unconventionally with comment, though that comment is fused with description to give us an initial image of David suffering from the chronic fatigue of depression, the rationale of which he logically summarizes later in the axiom "I'm tired because I'm bored and I'm bored because I hate working" (*NCW*, 50): "I sometimes think my tiredness is different from other people's. A different *kind* of thing. Once, I think it was in *Reader's Digest*, I saw the words *'depth fatigue'* and I'm pretty sure that's what I've got. Take the way I feel when I wake up in the morning. Apart from the specific things—dull headache, sore throat, inflamed eyelids and nausea—I feel chronically tired all over" (*NCW*, 49).

We next find out that he is seeing a psychiatrist, one Dr. Maximillian Cottle, with whom he is merely playacting out his sessions—the text has a scriptlike typographical appearance at one point (*NCW*, 52)—and we learn of his ironic reverse relationship with Dr. Cottle, an awareness of which raises the important question explored in the rest of the story of who is mad and who really sane: "Dr. Cottle interests me. The first few times I went he managed to control himself—he was using a Carl Rogers technique then— but the periods of silence seemed to eat his nerves raw. After a couple of visits I got a library book on Rogers and the non-directive method which gave me the whiphand. Since then, I've managed to bring him out quite a lot" (*NCW*, 50). We also gradually learn through these sessions what really happened in Wales that day David walked into the sea. But, what is more important, we learn why he went to Wales and why he cannot accept his world *"necessarily as it is"* (*NCW*, 54) and why, ironically, his date-stamped life, not his "impossible search for excuses" (*NCW*, 54), is "obviously impossible as a way of life" (NCW, 55) for him. Perhaps out of all the details he offers of the numbing routine of his daily existence, none is more epitomizing than the following:

"And," he said, "you have the future to think about." I *didn't* tell him to what extent the future *did* possess me; how it shadowed each passing day; because that was precisely what he didn't want to hear. I didn't tell him how I feared the future which is only my present repeated CLICK click CLICK repeated. I didn't tell him that if I rolled round the strips of rubber on the date-stamp I would age with them. In November, January, April or May, this year, next year, each and every year the library floor would still gleam with polish; Miss Nevins' slip would still be peeping from beneath her withered dress; the electric clock would still be humming through the endless afternoon and my life would still be slowly stamped away CLICK click CLICK of the date-stamp CLICK click CLICK stamping my life away two weeks from now two weeks from then two weeks from *then*. And fines for being late. (NCW, 55)

It is from this world that David wishes to escape when he boards a train for North Wales with no more deliberateness than the whimsical but unconscious symbolic lure of the pastoral, natural world represented by the poster outside the station showing the Welsh mountains and a stream. As opposed to the "click" of the date-stamp, the "click of the wheels and the clack-clacking of the knob of the window cord against the glass" (NCW, 56–57) echo his father's typing from the past and induce childhood memories of innocence and happiness identified with a pastoral, natural world—the very prelapsarian world that he is implicitly seeking through his flight (NCW, 57). He finds that innocent, free world again, only to lose it once more. Yet he will carry its image with him always.

Throughout the story David speaks parenthetically several times in sentences that constitute an internal substitutionary narrative of what is really happening or has happened in contrast to the surface narrative that Dr. Cottle is directing. But toward the end the real story breaks out of parentheses—for us if not for Dr. Cottle—initiated with the paragraph, "But behind my frank and honest eyes, quite safe from Dr. Maximillian Cottle, I treasured the gleaming sweep of the estuary; and louder than his questions the sound of gulls" (NCW, 59). What follows are four densely textured pages fusing description and report that constitute a vision of the beauty

and freedom of the natural world of the Welsh estuary—the title
of the story emblematizes the vision—on that wonderful evening
and subsequent morning, followed by the taste of the salt gift and
the mystical vision of the porpoises, epitomizing in his intuitive
understanding and response to them that beauty and freedom. The
section should be quoted in its entirety to do it justice.

In contrast to these intense pastoral images and all that they
imply are a series of cinematic images that signify metonymically
the raw, decrepit urban world from which David wishes to flee: "A
huddled figure on a municipal bench staring over the neat gravel
path and the trim lawn at the central bed of municipal flowers.
And near his feet a grey sea of pigeons heaving and fluttering over
a paper bag. The pigeons had horrid red feet—not pretty pink like
coral—raw, red like sores. Like the hands of the girl in the bus
queue" (*NCW*, 56). The pigeons contrast with the gulls of the
estuary, and the hands here are associated with those of the rheumatic
bus conductor mentioned earlier in the story. Both pairs of hands
are, in turn, identified with the hands of the final sentence of the
story, which begins with the coordinating conjunction "and" thus
signaling closure, even as the voices are distinguished from those
of the gulls and identified with Dr. Cottle's: "And the hands, the
hand and the voices guided me back to the beach" (*NCW*, 63).

## Chapter Three
# Initiation Stories

In the commentary that accompanies his two stories in *Sixteen by Twelve* Metcalf refers to a series of his stories "about youths and children and the process of growing up." He lists the following stories, which I have subdivided into three groups: a) "Biscuits," "The Tide Line," "Early Morning Rabbits"; b) "Keys and Watercress," "The Children Green and Golden," "A Thing They Wear"; and c) "Pretty Boy" and "A Bag of Cherries."[1] To this last category, three other relevant stories that Metcalf does not mention should be added: "I've Got It Made," "Our Mr. Benson," and "Beryl."

All these stories, in one way or another, confront the mysteries of mortality, time, age, society, nature, or sex. All of them utilize the pattern of an initiation narrative in which a character—usually but not always a child or adolescent—first learns a significant, even life-determining truth about the universe, reality, society, people, a particular person, or himself or herself. Such a subject matter tends to determine the main contours of the action of the story: it begins with the reflector in a state of innocence or mistaken belief, then leads up to the moment of illumination or the discovery of the truth, and ends usually with some indication of the consequences of that discovery, though whatever form the consequences take for the reflector may not be articulated but merely inferred by the reader. There may be perception inscribed in the text, in other words, not necessarily apperception. Sometimes, too, such stories end with a pseudo-epiphany that serves not so much to reveal something as to lead the reader back into the depths of the story, leaving him or her to reflect on the story more than to understand it. Generally, however, there is some implied if not articulated moment of illumination. Such a narrative line is "particularly suitable to a short story," as Jerome Beaty points out, "because it lends itself to brief treatment: the illumination is more or less sudden—there is no need for lengthy development, for multiple scenes or settings, for much time to pass, for too many complications of action or a large cast of characters—yet it can encapsulate a whole life or important segment of a life and wide-ranging, significant themes."[2]

In the stories of the first two subgroups, Metcalf concentrates on children, capturing the feel and texture of childhood perception and understanding superbly as the focalizers of these stories confront questions of identity, the natural world, death, sexuality, and adult power.

"Biscuits" is the first of the second-degree stories incorporated by the narrator into "The Teeth of My Father," a story to be examined in depth later, but, like the other inscribed stories in "The Teeth of My Father," it is meant to stand initially on its own. On the surface it is a simple piece of juvenilia, but it is an interesting story for several reasons. It is the first instance of an artist figure in Metcalf's fiction, a figure in both manifest and displaced forms that dominates Metcalf's later fiction, and it is a clear example of three overlapping components of Metcalf's poetic, which he articulates in the following remarks: "The emotional impulse of nearly all my stories is autobiographical; the events are not necessarily so at all"; "Many of my stories are a bringing together of passionately remembered physical detail and a re-ordering of the real into a new order which makes a new kind of real"; "If you can't give it a name, it's not there."[3] Language is not a mere nomenclature; it in fact names "things" into being, phenomenologically constituting our reality.

The intelligent and observant little boy we glimpse sitting in his mother's kitchen while she bakes, drawing biscuits with his crayons and counting and naming them by writing, is an embryonic artist. But he is also *"engaged in,"* as the somewhat pompous critical voice of "The Teeth of My Father" tells us, *"the act of defining his identity"* (*TMF,* 63) and his place in the world, especially evident in his writing down his complete address at the very end of the story (*TMF,* 63). Writing in itself identifies him with his father, who is, however, "far away in another part of the house" typing, as does his specific writing of his name "just above the rough place" (*TMF,* 62) where his father roughened the plaster of his false teeth. But he names other things into being too:

Outside under the snow there was the lawn and the rockery, and the stones along the edge of the path and the compost-heap in the corner by the fence, and the posts where the runner beans were where he'd seen the rat last summer, and the box by the garage with a hedgehog in it. And that was the stump of the elm tree. He recited each detail to himself, and as he named them his fingers curled under the window ledge to touch the secret place where the plaster was roughened. (*TMF*, 62)

The point of view is an internal third-person center of consciousness, and the substitutionary perception inscribed in the texture of the language here and elsewhere—diction and syntax—is authentically childlike, especially the effective use of polysyndeton, the repetition of conjunctions, above.

Although the point of view in "The Tide Line" is also a third-person center of consciousness, it is not consistently controlled. The focus is a child's, and the language is too except for the instances of the indirect discourse of his mother, which index her character, and of dialogue, but the voice is clearly the narrator's most of the time despite some passages of effective substitutionary perception. Metcalf lapses badly in the paragraph where Charles, the focalizer, discovers the world of nature along the tide line: "Mussell shells, painted tops, limpets tangled in streamers of seaweed, curving razor-shells . . . clusters of whelk eggs, the white shields of cuttlefish, mermaids' purses . . . jade-green ovals of sea-smoothed glass" (*LSF*, 115). This is what is known as paralepsis, presenting to the reader information that the prevailing level of focalization ought to render inaccessible. Now since Charles, like the little boy of "Biscuits," has already been established as a character struggling to understand the natural world by speaking, naming, spelling, and writing, he would not know the names of these "strange treasures" of the tide line. One purple sentence in this passage is particularly noticeable: "He stroked the driftwood branches which implored the air like drowning arms and fingers" (*LSF*, 115). This is not substitutionary perception but an invention of the narrator, who as a result no longer remains effaced.

Charles's response to the green lizard that he and his parents encounter on their way down to sunbathe on the beach at Bournemouth is an anticipation of his experience with the dead seagull. It elicits both excitement and fear, and its image—its neck, throat, color, eye—haunts him. His speaking aloud about lizards, echoing what his father has said, is a way of understanding the natural world through naming and thus of balancing his fear. His wish to record his father's words complements this notion, but it also suggests that

Charles, like the little boy of "Biscuits," is another embryonic artist in his wish to record his observations and growing knowledge. His pleasure in his new fourteen-carat gold pen, a gift from his father, both identifies him with his father, who is "copying figures from the newspaper with his silver propelling pencil" (*LSF*, 114), and reinforces his status as an embryonic artist, especially when he faces the sea to spell the two words he phonetically identifies: "C.A.R.A.T" and "C.A.R.R.O.T." (*LSF*, 115).

The story generates a tension between the authority of his mother—notice how frequently he asks permission to do something—and his free, wandering discoveries which will introduce him to another kind of authority. After he comes upon the "strange treasures" of the tide line, he encounters the carcass of a dead seagull. Just as he is about to reach out and touch the bird, "Suddenly, above him, a seabird's grating scream. The harsh sound echoed against the enclosing rock walls. He fell back and stared up into the sun, the black shape above him. The raucous cry sounded again, clamouring in his head. The bird slipped lower, filling in the sky with its black wings. Charles scrabbled away towards the rocks. He huddled into the shadow until he could feel the rock cutting into his back" (*LSF*, 116). Because the "iron cry" of the seabird evokes his guilt, he empties his pockets of the ovals of glass he had earlier picked up on the tide line, "flinging them down onto the sand and pebbles near the dead bird" (*LSF*, 116). He has encroached in some mysterious way on nature's territory.

He returns quickly from the white, black, and yellow world of the tide line to the orange of the beach, the green of the umbrella, and the red of his mother's bathing suit; but he does not join his parents. He remains instead on the line metaphorically poised between two orders, the sea and the sand, nature and civilization or society, drawing designs with the fingers of one hand and then smoothing them out and clutching with the other hand his fountain pen. Some epiphany is implied, some knowledge has been gained, even if it is not articulated. The clutching of the pen might suggest posteriority, the future action of recording what he has learned in his holiday book, and the drawing of and subsequent obliterating of designs on the sand might suggest the imposition of arbitrary human order on nature. Or does Charles clutch the fountain pen because it is his, because it gives him security, stability, identity, after what he has unsettlingly witnessed? It can, after all, easily be construed as a phallic symbol of patriarchal social order.

The ending of "The Tide Line" is much more open than any of those stories we have examined so far and that of "Early Morning Rabbits," the very first story that Metcalf wrote, another exploration of a child's confrontation with the natural world and of guilt. "Early Morning Rabbits" is the first story in the sequence "The Geography of Time," but Metcalf revised the story considerably for its publication in *The Lady Who Sold Furniture*. The changes are instructive, for all of them are attempts to pare down, to move the story more toward the inferential and synecdochic, to move it away from "telling" and more toward "showing." There nevertheless remains a noticeable amount of ornateness, and similes in particular are, perhaps unwittingly, foregrounded: "The hens, anxious to climb inside the shed, clustered in falling pyramids like the acrobats at the Hippodrome" (*LSF*, 104); the eel "began to writhe its body like a length of conjuror's rope, glistening knots tying and untying, its belly a startling white-blue, excrement squeezing from its vent like dirty toothpaste" (*LSF*, 106); "The fields, the grass, the trees and bushes were all mysteriously still as if everything was a model or as if the enemy had sprayed the earth with a paralysing gas" (*LSF*, 108).

The point of view is a third-person center of consciousness with not as much of a gap between focus and voice for the effaced narrator to be heard, though we certainly hear him distinctly in the similes quoted above. The substitutionary perception within this consciousness is especially effective in rendering sensory perception—sight and smell in particular—and emotional facets as we witness young David's response to the unaccustomed rural environment of his aunt's and uncle's farm which he is visiting on holiday. He is about to lose one kind of innocence, to be fully initiated into the horrifying natural world of wounding and death in his shooting of the rabbit.

Two flashbacked incidents, one an iterative scene and one a singulative scene,[4] both serve as foreshadowings of the guilt and horror he will experience in his confrontation with the rabbit. The first concerns "a long knife with a strange fat blade and a black handle that was used for killing pigs" (*LSF*, 104): "When his uncle was off in the bottom fields, he sometimes went into the warm gloom of the shed and took the knife down and stabbed sacks with it, saying to himself, *This knife has killed pigs*, and he would imagine his uncle stabbing it again and again into the fat pig in the yard, and then put it back because he felt wrong" (*LSF,* 104). The second concerns the eel he had caught on his nightlines but about which he does not tell his uncle because he implicitly feels guilt (*LSF,* 106–7). The rabbit, too, its eye like the eel's eye, will seek him out, confronting him, accusing him in its wounded brownness, as he eyes, stands staring at, the horror of what he has done:

His eyes came back to the brown body. He could hardly believe what he saw. . . . The seeping eye seemed to grow, spreading in a viscous pool, blotting out the fringe of trees and the stone wall and the crooked hawthorn tree, growing in its wounded brownness till it filled the world.
The squealing, the sound of chalk on board or scraping fingernails.
And the running, running legs of the still body. (*LSF,* 110)

The masculine rhyme of "squealing" and "running" and the repetition of "running," the figure epizeuxis (the repetition of a word with no other word in between), in ironic contrast to the "still body" suggests the pursued feeling David will experience as his guilt spreads and blots out his world. An epiphany is implied, though this time, unlike in "The Tide Line," it is much less inarticulate, especially since beginning the final sentence with " And" signals closure.

The next three stories—"Keys and Watercress," "The Children Green and Golden," and "A Thing They Wear"—involve the child's confrontation with adult perspectives and values. All three revolve around a subtle awareness of sexuality, the last more explicitly than the first two, and all three are part of the same fictional world.

"Keys and Watercress" opens with a scenic report that establishes immediately the imagistic (metonymic and metaphoric) signifiers of sexuality by which the story moves as we glimpse, through a third-person center of consciousness, another young David, this time fishing in a river:

David, with great concentration, worked the tip of his thumbnail under the fat scab on his knee. He carefully lifted the edges of the scab enjoying the tingling sensation as it tore free. His rod was propped against his other leg and he could just see the red blur of his float from the corner of his eye. He started to probe the centre of the crust.
"Had any luck?" a voice behind him said suddenly.

Startled, his thumbnail jumped, ripping the scab away. A bright bead
of blood welled into the pit. The sun, breaking from behind the clouds,
swept the meadow into a brighter green and made the bead of blood glisten
like the bezel of a ring.
    "Had any luck?" the old man said again. David twisted round to look
at him. He wasn't in uniform and he wasn't wearing a badge and anyway
he was far too old to be a bailiff. Unless he was a Club Member—and
they could report you too. And break your fishing rod.
    David glanced down the river towards the bridge and the forbidding
white sign. "I'm only fishing for eels," he said. "With a seahook." (*LSF*,
118–19)

The notions of pain and pleasure, scabs, blood, eels, and rod all
have sexual connotations; and the specific reference to a wound, a
"pit," anticipates the wound, the "pit,"of the old man who, after
he has invited David back to his house for tea, tries to get David
to put his finger into the "pit" of his leg made by a rifle "ball."
The old man's concern about the names of things and about taste,
texture, and vision, as well as his maxims such as "always be at-
tentive. Always accumulate *facts*" (*LSF*, 122), while they function
as an index of his eccentric character, are also implicit directives for
the reader. Consider, for example, the old man's bizarre behavior
and vicariously erotic joy when he buries his hands in his exotic
collection of keys (keys being a commonplace Freudian image of the
phallus) and throws them wildly: "His breathing was loud and
shallow. He looked up at David, and his eyes widened. 'Now!' he
shouted, and heaved his hands into the air" (*LSF*, 126). Afterwards,
"The old man remained bent across the table as if the excitement
had exhausted him" (*LSF*, 126). Notice the use of "as if," a locution
that allows for meaningful ambiguity. It may be simple exhaustion,
but it may be something else too.
    In entering the house, David, as the descriptive details meto-
nymically suggest, moves from the ouside light of innocence into
the dark, enclosing presence of experience. After the keys episode,
during which the heavy red velvet curtains had been drawn because,
as the old man says suggestively, "we don't want to be overlooked"
(*LSF*, 124), David asks to have the curtains opened and is refused.
The old man is identified with decrepitude and the smell of urine,
and as the room grows even darker during the bullet pit incident,
the crowding presence of the old man, "his black shape" (*LSF*, 128),
looms over David:

The old man moved even nearer to the settee, and leaning forward over David, lifting with his hands, slowly raised his leg until his foot was resting on the cushion. The harsh wheezing of his breath seemed to fill the silent room. The smell of stale urine was strong on the still air. Slowly he began to tug at his trouser-leg, inching it upwards. The calf of his leg was white and hairless. The flesh sank deep, seamed and puckered, shiny, livid white and purple, towards a central pit.

"If you press hard," said the old man, "it sinks right in."

David shrank further away from the white leg. The old man reached down and grasped David's hand. "Give me your finger," he said. (*LSF*, 159)

This is an epanaleptic echo of the beginning of the story, and the very end reports David's panicked departure, indicating closure, as does the negation in the old man's remark as he yells after him, "But you have *no appreciation*" (*LSF*, 129).

The title of "The Children Green and Golden" comes, of course, from Dylan Thomas's well-known poem, "Fern Hill" (1.44), an epitomizing pastoral image of prelapsarian, "lordly," innocent "lamb white days." (Metcalf claims that Thomas's exotic style had an insidious effect upon his early writing, particularly in the lushness of a story like "Early Morning Rabbits.")[5] Joyce Cary's *A House of Children* is also a related text. The intertextual relationship between the story and these other texts imbues it with a considerable amount of added thematic significance, reminding us that all texts are re-iterative and borderless, as we follow the playful activities of three green and golden boys—David, Peter, and Rory—for a few days of their young lives on the beach at Bournemouth. The predominant mode of the story is speech, and the point of view is third-person internal—that is, the vehicle of the story is an unpersonalized narrator-focalizer from within the locus of represented events, not a character focalizer—an entirely appropriate form of mediation given the story's concern with the responses of three children, not merely one, and with this focalized object primarily from without and only a bit from within.

The boys are on the edge of adolescence and on the edge of sexual awareness, evident in their boyish prank of yelling "Give her a big belly!" (*NCW*, 6) to a young couple they come upon on the beach in intimate but innocent repose after having glimpsed the "white bulge" (*NCW*, 5) of the girl's breast, and even more evident in their disturbed feelings about Rory's mother, reported in the beginning of the story, when they have to call at Rory's house: "David waited outside the gate while Pete went up the stairs to the front door. They didn't like going to Rory's house because his mother was funny. She always said things like, 'So you are Rory's little friends,' and she never seemed to get dressed. She was always wearing a nightdress and her toe-nails were bright red. Rory's father had gone away. Rory used to steal money from her purse and one day he had watched her through the keyhole when she was having a bath" (*NCW,* 3). A sexual motif asserts itself, too, toward the end of the story when they symbolically destroy the pen of the evangelical Uncle Michael, an obvious phallic symbol of power. But the sexual motif only simmers beneath the surface of the narrative, for the story's main concern is with the tension between childhood innocence, its natural interests, and imposed adult conceptions and values.

The religious and moral concerns of Uncle Michael and Auntie Mary in their "Suffer the Children Campaign" are meaningless to children whose interest, simply because they are children, is naturally elsewhere—with squirrels, fish, swifts, swallows, gulls, polar hawks, and hawkmoth caterpillars. Uncle Michael and Auntie Mary are really bribing the children with their reward system of games and religious prizes, playing on their concerns as boys, and the children attend the campaign only because they want the badges and to fill up the albums with cards for their own sake, not because of their religious significance whose meaning is lost upon the boys. The irony of this situation and the meaning of that irony are dramatized in the juxtaposition of snatches of Uncle Michael's recitation of the parable of the sower and the boys' distraction and concern with the caterpillar. An additional irony resides in the fact that the boys might be considered examples of the meaning of the parable.

Rory's theft of Uncle Michael's pen is in itself ironic, too, in light of Uncle Michael's didactic efforts; and Rory's obsessive need to destroy the pen, in whose destruction he is joined by the other two boys, is an implicit reaction to authority, a libidinal release of pent-up hostility, a mock destruction of adult power represented phallically by the pen.

The story ends with a reassertion of nature as "lordly" as it epanaleptically echoes—technically the figure is polyptoton, repetition with a difference—metonymic details from earlier in the story:

Rory rolled off into the warm sand and pillowed his head on his hands. David propped himself up and lighted a cigarette. The heat seemed to roll in waves. High up against the sandstone cliff the black shapes of the swallows flickered like the blink of an eyelash. With a sigh of contentment, David unbuttoned his shirt and settled down to let the warmth soak through him. Swimming in the darkness behind his closed eyes were gentle globes of light, red and glowing.

    Pete said, "We could try for those swallow-nests this afternoon."

    "Swifts," mumured David.

    "Swallows."

    "Mmmm," sighed David happily. (*NCW*, 20)

"The heat seemed to roll in waves. High up against the sandstone cliff the black shapes of the swallows flickered like the blink of an eyelash"—these two sentences occur in reverse order shortly after the emotional release following the encounter with the lovers (*NCW*, 6–7),[6] and there as here David strips away his clothing, a traditional metaphor of civilization as distinct from the natural. These are indeed the children green and golden before they follow time "out of grace" (1. 45).

In "A Thing They Wear" we see the beginning of that journey from the grace of childhood innocence to the deflating reality of adult experience in the boy's witnessing of a woman's changing of her sanitary napkin, in their disturbing discovery—to use their language that echoes the emblematic title—of "a sort of thing they wear" (*TMF*, 110). Although the story focuses more on one of the two characters, David, than on the other, Rory, the point of view is not a third-person center of consciousness but, again, an internal unpersonalized narrator-focalizer: the story is concerned with the behavioral response of more than one character, but told from within the locus of narrated events. The focus on the two boys, however, is once more from without, not from within, a technique that is a very effective strategy because it demands a more intense inference of meaning from the reader. As in "The Children Green and Golden," focalization from without is entirely appropriate, too, because the objects of focalization are children whose apperceptions, unlike their perceptions which can be handled in substitutionary perception, are more difficult to render in terms of their language and conceptual limitations.

The story begins with a scenic report of David's and Rory's re-
trieving of some packets of dummy cigarettes from the dustbins
behind a tobacconist's shop. Smoking used to be, of course—maybe
still is for the ill-informed—an aping of, an attempt to be initiated
into, manhood. With their real smoking, then, and their pretense
of smoking the dummies, they pretend to be adults, but the joke
they intend to play with the dummies on their parents and teachers,
while it indirectly indicates their desire to be adults, also mocks
that adult world. After their discovery of "a thing they wear," as
the story narrows in to focus on David, we see that he at least is
not really ready for the rites of passage into manhood, though he
has taken an irretrievable step toward it.

There are several anticipations or preparations for this deflation,
for the fact that he is still a child: David's implicit fear of the
authority of his father in his discussion of the joke with Rory (*TMF*,
103); their abrupt breaking off of their mocking song about one of
their teachers, "Happy Carterstein" (*TMF*, 105); David's wish to
look older and to dress as Rory, evidence of both his wish to be an
adult and a reminder that he is after all still a child (*TMF*, 105).
Other reminders that David is still a child are his ordering of "two
banana ices" when Rory buys five Woodbine cigarettes (*TMF*, 106)
and, finally, his holding of his cigarette "carefully so as not to get
any yellow on his fingers" (*TMF*, 108).

The idyllic childhood state from which the boys are about to fall
is explicitly identified with a pastoral retreat in the metonymic
setting of "the holly tree in the middle of the wood"—a typological
image of another tree in another wood, the tree of knowledge in
Eden—when they make their puzzled discovery:

The boys stood silent in the gloomy hollow. A hover-fly hung over the
floor of dead leaves, the slight whine of its wings the only sound in the
silence. Then Rory flipped the white thing over with his foot.
"I wonder why it's got blood on it," said David.
"I dunno," said Rory, shrugging his shoulders and turning away to climb
up the bank. (*TMF*, 110–11)

Notice the gloom, the silence, the hover-fly (analogously Beelzebub,
lord of the flies),[7] and David's immediate retreat into childhood
subservience:

"Coming?"

"Yes," said David suddenly. "Yes, I'd better be getting home. I've got to be back at half-past four."

"Okay," said Rory. "See you tonight, then."

"Yes. If she'll let me out." (*TMF*, 111)

Immediately after this exchange, the effaced narrator steps forward to tell us what David does not do on his way home from the wood, such a departure from his habitual behavior and characteristic perceptive ability indicating not only how disturbing the discovery is but also the vitiation of childhood sensibility (*TMF*, 111).

It is a descriptive report that contrasts vividly with an earlier section describing the boys' prelapsarian journey to the wood (*TMF*, 104). When David finally reaches home, we see him in a completely subdued condition, accepting his mother's reprimands for his still childlike behavior and either unwilling or unable to play the planned game with the cigarettes. The negation in his answer to his father's question, "Where did you get those cigarettes?" "They're only dummies" (*TMF*, 112) signals closure.

The next four stories—"I've Got It Made," "Pretty Boy," "Our Mr. Benson," and "Beryl" are all concerned, to varying degrees, with the question of class in British society, and together with "A Bag of Cherries" all are concerned with the initiation of late adolescents into other worlds, other values.

The uncollected story, "I've Got It Made," is a lightweight piece that tells, through a third-person center of consciousness, of a middle-class adolescent boy's encounter with a "rehabilitated" working-class juvenile criminal during one day of his school vacation while he is working picking peas. There is a slight Dickensian flavor to the story, especially in the way in which speech indexes character in Tom, the recent graduate of "The Bad Boys College," Borstal. Speech is, in fact, the dominant mode of the story.

It is the difference between the two boys that moves the story: the kind of clothes they wear, the cigarettes they smoke, the language they use, the knowledge they have or lack, and Tom's tattoo.[8] The title is repeated twice, once about two-thirds of the way into the story and once at the end. Both uses, stressing the differences between the two boys, are ironic because of the pathos they engender: "I'm getting a room of my own in town. Crafton Street. Know it? Twelve and six a week. It isn't bad. Better than a dormitory anyway. And I might get regular work next week, see, in a garage. Then if I get that, I got it made"; "Tom held the green pound note and two half-crowns and the sixpence in his hand and grinned at David. 'When I get my room mate' —he chinked the half-crowns together—'I got it made.' "[9] How sad this boy really is. How little some will settle for.

Although "Pretty Boy" is no more interesting thematically than "I've Got It Made," it is a more substantial story, especially because of the subtlety of its imagistic patterns and its satiric impulse, the latter a mode that Metcalf will develop into a strength. The point of view a third-person center of consciousness, "Pretty Boy" is also an encounter between two boys: Allan, the son of a cleric, who wishes to enter a romantic, bohemian world emblematized in the coffeehouse Danse Macabre, and Eric, a boy Allan meets in the coffeehouse, who pretends to be of that world but is at heart just as middle-class as Allan. The bohemian world is in itself ersatz, the story's satiric impulse and ideology suggest, and the world represented by the Danse Macabre is every bit as arbitrary and clichéd as the middle-class homes from which the two boys come.

Allan, for instance, carries Joyce's *Ulysses* to the coffeehouse as a prop and removes his print of Van Gogh's *Sunflowers* from his bedroom wall and replaces it with a print of a Picasso nude only because "his older brother had come back from Cambridge one term and said that 'Van Gogh was passé, pure Woolworths" ' (*LSF*, 133). Besides sounding the ersatz theme, this arbitrary changing of prints echoes in the metonymic descriptive details about prints and other ersatz items at the coffeehouse: "Scythes, a plastic skeleton, and an enormous plastic hourglass suspended from the ceiling, decorated the *Danse Macabre*. On every table sat ashtrays shaped like skulls. Behind the counter were three yellowing bullfight posters left over from the days when the *Danse Macabre* had been called *El Matador*. The tattered menus were headed *The Matto Grosso*" (*LSF*, 133). These images, in turn, harken back to Allan's mother's taking down of the print of the Picasso nude and to her daffodil-patterned tea service and arrangement of sandwiches at the beginning of the story, both actions and descriptions metonymically suggesting her middle-class sensibilities and values (*LSF*, 131,130).

Allan is another Metcalfian embryonic artist, and he is also a sexually conscious young man, a condition evident in his series of revised sentences generated by his remembrance of "Sally" and her suede panties, by his persistent questioning of Eric about the waitress Carol, and by the poem he writes after the passage of substitutionary perception filled with romantic, erotic clichés about Carol (*LSF*, 132, 134).

When Eric and Christopher arrive at the Danse Macabre, we are treated to several pages of ironic, satiric dialogue of a pseudoreligious, pseudophilosophical tenor, and there is a heavy irony in Allan's admiration of Eric's presumed social superiority. The irony becomes intense once Allan and Eric arrive at Eric's house, to which they have repaired so that Eric may lend Allan copies of the *Vedas* and *Bhagavad-Vita*. Consider, for example, the irony of Eric's remark as they enter the house, "Wipe your feet cause there's a new carpet on the stairs" (*LSF*, 140), given that one of the dominant themes of his conversation is the repudiation of materialism. His blue budgerigar who says "Pretty Boy! Pretty Boy!"—which gives the story its title—and his hobby of model aircraft construction suggest the merely fashionable adolescent whimsy of his so-called interest in Eastern philosophy, suggest that he is in fact just an ordinary English bourgeois. The bird and the "two plastic cups" (*LSF*, 141) in its cage are metonymic signifiers of Eric's real condition: he is still encaged in his middle-class structures. Reiterating the ersatz theme, the plastic cups echo the other metonymic signifiers of plastic in the Danse Macabre: "the pink plastic spoon, the black plastic salt and pepper pots" (*LSF*, 136), the "plastic skeleton," and the "enormous plastic hourglass suspended from the ceiling" (*LSF*, 133). The final irony of the story is Eric's answer to Allan's question of "Where will I see you to give the book back?": "You can try the *Macabre*," called Eric. "If I haven't moved on" (*LSF*, 142). We know absolutely that he is not going to move on.

The humor in "Pretty Boy" is veiled in spite of the satiric impulse of the story, but in "Our Mr. Benson," it displays itself in wonderful plainness through the first-person speech of a narrator whom we know only as "Boy," the form of address he is accorded by his older coworker in the Leicester Co-operative Bakery, George Benson. As the title suggests, the voice of the narrator is shaped by a working-class communal perspective, and both the straightforward narrated sections of report and description and the dialogue ring with utter authenticity. Speech also indexes character—in particular the boy and Benson—brilliantly and humorously in the colloquial diction, the rhythms, accents, idioms, and syntax of the language.

Focusing on innocence versus experience, the story shows us the
boy's initiation into the skills of diplomacy necessary to deal with
management as he witnesses our Mr. Benson's crafty manipulation
of Piggy Bank's idea for improving the time it takes to pack up
the bakery orders. Metcalf is, of course, caricaturing the English
worker, the union man, in Benson's subtle sabotage of Bank's scheme,
but it is an affectionate stance, not, as in some of his later fictions
where caricature and grotesque are predominant, a savage one. The
story ends with an implied epiphany, the suggestion that the boy
has gained in awareness.

"Beryl" is a later story from the same fictional world as "Our
Mr. Benson" that deals with another variation of the theme of
innocence confronting experience through the encounter between
middle-class David, a university student working at the Leicester
Co-operative Bakery during his vacation, and working-class Beryl,
a young full-time worker in the fancy cakes building. The binary
opposition between the two classes is explored in terms of geo-
graphical, educational, cultural, social, and moral differences as
David descends from the shelter of middle-class order and values
into the vulgar reality of working-class manners and mores through
his romantic infatuation with Beryl.

A descent or deflation motif controls the major imagistic movements of the story from beginning to end. Notice, for example, the
opening image with its anaphora, a movement *down* and *away* from
David's trimmed, enclosed, blank, suburban environment (a metonym for moral, social, and cultural values) where the streets have
names like Laburnum Drive, Forsythia Avenue, and Laurel Grove
to the open "traffic" and "crowd" of the working-class world: "At
five a.m. it was still dark in the sleeping house and in stocking feet
David would drink a cup of coffee before making sandwiches and
filling a thermos. By 5:30, he would be walking down the hill in
loud boots, the street lights still bright under the paling sky, away
from the blank suburban houses with their lawns and rockeries
behind trim privet hedges, down towards the traffic of the main
road where he would join the crowd of workmen at the bus stop."
In the next paragraph we learn that "He enjoyed wearing the heavy
boots and being called 'skip' or 'chief' by the conductor" because
"it gave him a feeling of solidarity" (*TMF*, 113). But, by the end
of the story, he will discover in his final descent, his final deflation,
that he is an alien in this world. We are prepared for this final

deflation by the contrasting normative pastoral images that occur throughout the story—on the very first page, for example—and by the narrator's summary of anterior behavior, an unusual narrative device in Metcalf (*TMF,* 116). Although the focus is generally internal—we see things from David's point of view from within the locus of narrated events—the voice is not always David's but the narrator's. When this happens, the point of view drifts into an external stance.

The first major scene revealing David's alienated condition is the iterative report of how his afternoons are spent:

It was in the fancy cakes building that he worked until clocking-out at five. The building housed two long work benches and half a dozen machines. There he folded up boxes from the stacks of flat, slit cardboard, packed cakes, and heat-sealed packets of cellophane-wrapped tarts with an electric treadle machine. He was the only male. It was days before he could control his blushes through the long afternoons. Walking along the benches to distribute the made up boxes and gather the cartons of jam tarts was to run the gauntlet.
"Isn't he lovely?" one would say.
"Bet he's as tender as a young carrot," another would reply.
"Like to fill my box, would you, love?"
Of old Annie, who wept silently as she worked, they'd say,
"Doesn't wear nothing under her overall since you was put on."
When Greg, the electrician, came through, he'd yell to the machinists,
"Any of you girls need an adjustment?"
And they would shriek with laughter.
"Hark at 'im!"
"It'd take a bigger man than you." (*TMF,* 114–15)

Speech, of course, indexes both character and class here, and it is in this world that David discovers, through his adolescent infatuation with the sensual, the lovely Beryl:

Greg, the electrician, seemed to be one of her favorites.
"Come to fix my machine, Greg?"
"I wouldn't mind," he'd say.
Or flipping the row of screwdrivers he wore in the breast pocket of his brown overalls, she'd say,
"Always rely on Greg to have the proper tool."
And Greg would say,
"You'd be surprised, young Beryl, at all my apparatus."

"Why?" she'd say. "Got flashing lights on it, has it?" . . .

On the slow bus journeys, eating lunch and dinner, working and sleeping, images of Beryl burned in his mind. Beryl smiling, laughing, listening attentively to him, bending in her straining overall, teasing, Beryl undressing. He gave himself no rest. Yet, not knowing what to say or how to say it, and fearing rebuff, he could not bring himself to approach her beyond a casual nod or smile in the progress of the day. (*TMF*, 115–16)

He finally does encounter her face to face, but ironically through his knowledge of the natural world represented by the rare Camberwell Beauty he spots, the butterfly a detail identified with the pastoral images of the story.

Among the several details of her working-class background, which contrasts sharply to his, about which we learn through indirect discourse on their first date, we are told of her so-called interest in art. Because of this interest, David later gives her a Chinese scroll painting of "Two ducks on a river bank, three or four dark strokes of reeds, in the background the suggestion of a mountain"; but, alas, Beryl's taste ironically runs only to photographic realism: "I do like the mountains like you say, and those reeds *are* clever, but I like the ducks best. You could nearly touch them, couldn't you?" (*TMF*, 123). Walking home the ten miles that night of their first date, he recalls "*her* wanton touch at the back door," and this thought sets off riotous "rehearsals" in his mind of Beryl "ranging from the perverse to the pastoral" (*TMF*, 122), which set us up for the contrastive, squalid, vulgar reality of his actual sexual encounter with her on their next but last date.

When the films at the Roxy are over, during which they have been passionately "Clasped in the darkness," David discovers that he is "suffering the double pain of a prolonged erection and the desire to urinate" (*TMF*, 126). But at that moment, Beryl suggests that they "could go round to our gran's":

"What for?"
She held out a ring of keys.
"You mean . . . ?"
"Come on, she said. "It's not far." (*TMF*, 126)

Thus begins his final descent from Romance to Realism, "down" and even farther "away"—all the descriptive details, like those at the beginning of the story echoed here, are metonymic signifiers—

toward the squalid and working-class world. As twilight metonym-ically fades into night, "She led him away from the Roxy, away from the shops and traffic towards that part of the city where the streets were still cobbled and the hosiery mills and shoe factories stood black and massive against the sky. They turned down mean side streets and turned again until she indicated an archway. David found himself in a square courtyard, the backs of houses on all sides. Washing-lines criss-crossed the yard, a pair of sheets strange in the gloom. In the cobbled centre stood a row of outhouses" (*TMF*, 126).

Inside, she switches on the television to occupy him while she goes upstairs, an action that allows him to fantasize what she is doing: "He wondered what she was doing upstairs. Sitting silent, perhaps, in front of a mirror. Perhaps unpinning and brushing the lustre of her hair. Dabbing perfume behind her ears and on her throat from a precious and long-hoarded vial. Plumping pillows, smoothing back the sheets, unbuttoning her frock. In a few moments she would call him and he would go up to her" (*TMF*, 127). Like his previous sexual fantasies of Beryl, this sets us up for the deflation that follows immediately, and the ironic juxtaposition between the "Three Anglican vicars . . . discussing modern attitudes to mir-acles" (*TMF*, 127) on the television and David's awkward fondling of Beryl is ludicrously comic, but not as bizarre as the juxtaposition between the gangster film to which she switches and what happens next:

"Come on," she breathed against his cheek.
Gunfire sounded from the TV. Windows broke. Police were speaking through a loud-hailer advising the occupants they were surrounded.
Her hand was working its way inside his underpants.
"What's the matter?" she said.
"Nothing."
*Thud. Thud-thud. Thud.*
He started. The noise came from the ceiling, from the room above.
"Come *on*," she said, pushing, pushing herself against him, her frock bunched above her waist. One arm tightened round his shoulders.
"What's wrong?" she repeated.
*Thud. Thud-thud-thud.*
"What *is* that?" he said, rearing away.
"It's only our gran," said Beryl.
The remnant of his erection wilted.

"It's alright," she said, sitting up. "She's bedrid. Just wants a cup of tea, I expect."

She lay back on the carpet.

Kneeling, David looked at her spread hair. On the screen, a braced and straddled man was being frisked by a police officer.

"I can't," he said.

She lay still for a moment staring up at him and then with a heave, a snap of elastic, she got to her feet shaking down her frock.

"Well," she said. "I'd better make our gran a cup of tea, then." (*TMF*, 128–29)

Notice the implied connection in the juxtaposition of "her spread hair" and the "straddled" criminal as David is struck by the "thud-thud-thud," and his wilted erection, of course, is an emblem of the whole deflating experience. The story ends with his departure and her implicit wish to be free of him, the negation of the final sentence a convention that announces closure: " 'All I wish is,' she said, 'you hadn't given me those ducks' " (*TMF*, 130).

The fusion of humor and pathos here and elsewhere in "Beryl" is characteristic of many of Metcalf's stories. So are the exploration of class consciousness and the fantasizing and artist motifs. In "A Bag of Cherries," for instance, a story that "explores the sadness of the generation gap," David, a student traveling home on a train from university, fantasizes about a young woman passenger as a springboard to re-create his "story," his obsessive fantasy "that on a journey, on a train, hitchhiking perhaps, he'd meet a rich, lonely young woman of taste and sophistication."[10] The fantasy, a marvellous instance of hypotyposis,—that is, a description of people and events that exist in imagination only—is richly textured in subtly humorous metonymic signifiers:

But her room! A deep, black carpet. White walls. Rich saffron curtains reaching to the floor. Commanding and stark against the white walls, set within niches, primitive carvings from the Congo. On the wall above the couch a Byzantine Christ on a wood panel.

As she refilled the wine glasses, he wandered over to the Sheraton table and glanced at the books lying there. One, bound in green crushed Morocco, was a privately printed and illustrated edition of Huysman's *A Rebours*. The other, in a white bible binding and blind-stamped with a cross, was DeSade's *Les crimes de l'amour*.

A subtle fragrance of incense, light and dry like the wine, scented the
air . . .
    Candle light. The whisper of silk . . . (*ST,* 181)

As his fantasy suggests, David imagines himself as an artist—"a
rejection," Metcalf says in his comments on the story in *Sixteen by
Twelve* "of the middle-class life style summed up in the account of
the mother's letter. [11] Filled with brilliant metonymic signifiers of
his mother's habitual behavior, the letter is an example of both
indirect and—because it is imagined—virtual speech that indexes
character superbly (*ST,* 182). Despite the differences between David
and his mother, their attitude toward love and sex, for example,
David is inextricably a part of her. His obsessive checking that his
suitcase is secure in the luggage rack, for instance, identifies him,
as he annoyingly realizes, with his mother, who is always double-
checking gas taps on the stove before going to sleep.

He is even more closely identified with his father despite the
barrier of his father's priestliness, as we see in the "treasured memory" of the outing with his father, the wonder of that mythological
childhood day emblematized in the title by the bag of cherries David
and his father share as they walk through a village and over the
moors in Yorkshire. The perfection of that day of oneness between
father and son is also emblematized in the sun "perfect with rays
like a child's drawing, and the sun was stuck right in the middle
of a sky, a sky of the purest blue" (*ST,* 183). But what is most
significant about that day is that David's father is not wearing the
black suit and white collar of his calling, "the suggestion that their
happiness on that day results from the father's release from the
priestly role. The father, like David, wipes his hands on his trousers.
He also helps David carry home the treasure—'the shining cartridge
cases.' "[12]

When David first glimpses his father after getting off the train,
he "felt a sudden surge of excitement and pleasure but, not knowing
why he did so, pretended not to have seen him" (*ST,* 184). This
response is anticipated in an earlier substitutionary perception, "But
although going home was not exactly an adventure, he always felt
an anticipation, in spite of himself, a sense of excitement" (*ST,*
183). He feels excited and happy both because he implicitly loves
his father and because it is to his happy past that he is metaphorically
returning. What follows this moment, however, is a deterioration

into inconsequential dialogue and silence, as the treasured memory of the outing contrasts starkly with the petty reality of the conversation between father and son. The story winds down to a final couple of sentences that in the sense of closure signaled epitomize the mundaneness of the small talk between the two:

"Ah, well," said his father, "I expect you'll be about ready for a cup of tea."

"Yes," said David, staring at his father's profile, "a cup of tea would be very nice" (*ST*, 185).

# Chapter Four
# Art and Artists

The richly textured stories in *The Teeth of My Father* are among Metcalf's best and most interesting, particularly the first five, which constitute a self-contained sequence: "The Strange Aberration of Mr. Ken Smythe," "The Practice of the Craft," "Gentle as Flowers Make the Stones," "The Years in Exile," and "The Teeth of My Father." The five stories were all written over a period of a year and a half, but they were not consciously planned as a related group of stories. Presumably, they are merely the cumulative products of Metcalf's thematic preoccupations during a certain period of time. They do, nevertheless, form a self-contained sequence. Demonstrating Metcalf's evolution into Canadian-set material, all five stories are concerned in different ways with different aspects of the same dilemma: the plight of the artist in terms of either the relationship between the artist and society or the relationship between the artist's execution of his craft and his own personal life. If we arrange the stories in the order given above, which is not the order in which they appear in the book, the movement from the first to the fifth story reveals a progressive internalization and particularization of the artist's predicament. For example, the first story, "The Strange Aberration of Mr. Ken Smythe," metaphorically dramatizes the artist's tenuous relationship to society and, through the ultimately hostile and unappreciative audience that witnesses the performance by the boys' brass band, suggests the essentially vulnerable position of the artist vis-à-vis his community. The fourth story in this arrangement, "The Years in Exile," through a first-person persona who is a novelist, explores the built-in tension of an artist's life in terms of a division within the artist's mind in that the narrator's memories of his childhood in England—because he has fictionalized the past—are more real to him than his present moment in Canada as a famous novelist. The artist figures in the first four stories represent any artist who is obliged to live in the real world but create idealized objects. The fifth story, "The Teeth of My Father," although it deals generally with the relationship between factual and fictional truth, focuses on Metcalf's own concerns as an artist or writer and on the relationship between his own life and his own fiction.

As in many of Metcalf's stories, there is a strong satiric vein, which often verges on outright savage ridicule, in "The Strange Aberration of Mr. Ken Smythe." The story moves on a bitterly humorous level; but it is, on a more subtle, almost allegorical level, a story about an artistic event—the performance by a German boys' band, called "The International Amity Boys Brass Band," at the Municipal Entertainments in the Pleasure Gardens of Edinburgh on a certain summer evening. Both the words "International" and "Amity" take on ironic significance as we move through the story, for Metcalf has deliberately established an extreme situation in which the audience is anything but an elite coterie and in which there are likely to be racial and nationalistic prejudices involved in the response to the band's performance, a circumstance intensified by having the Glasgow Variety Show precede the Essen Brass Band. We are immediately alerted to the potential conflict by the descriptive detail in the first paragraph of the metonymic iconic opposition between "the massive War memorial" and "the Pleasure Gardens" (*TMF*, 7). The attitude toward the artist is frankly elitist and somewhat romantic. It is an unqualified sympathetic view, increased by the fact that the members of the band are merely boys, one of whom, Heine, is symbolically attacked as artist when he is physically wounded by "a stone, a bottle, something thrown from the darkness" of the audience (*TMF*, 21). There is no sense of narratorial irony about the artist here: Metcalf simply does not choose to explore the irony of the artist's choice to be an artist.

The point of view is a cameralike third-person focus, at first moving but then fixed. Everything is seen through the eyes of an anonymous onlooker, an unpersonalized traveler, but while it is technically an internal focus in that the locus of focalization is inside the represented events, the voice—because it is a cameralike focus—is the narrator's. The selection of details, the value judgments made, and the feelings and attitudes are presumably those of the traveler, and the object of focalization—the various performances on stage and the behavior of the audience—is seen from without, not within. But Metcalf does not really circumscribe the perceptual ability of the traveler. There is, in fact, an absolute coincidence between the traveler's views and the narrator's, for the purpose of the anonymous traveler is solely to establish a rhetorical stance of presumed objectivity and detachment. The third-person point of view is a disguise, "a mask worn by the text for its own rhetorical purposes."[1] Had Metcalf used a first-person point of view, for example, the credibility of the sordid context in which the artistic performance takes place would have been questionable. Actually, the point of view is analogous to the relationship between a director and his camera in a film. The traveler's perceptions and apperceptions are the camera: where he looks and on what he focuses—value judgments in themselves—are determined by the narrator. The analogy is not inappropriate, for there is an obvious sense of cinematography in the story—a constant shifting of angles of vision from the stage to the audience, focusing on a part of that audience, the American family; back to the stage, focusing on a part of the band; et cetera—and, as in film, as the narrative becomes increasingly more tense and dramatic, the reader's awareness of the particular point of view (that is, that these are the observations of the traveler) diminishes. The point of view has really modulated into what Seymour Chatman calls nonnarrated dramatic focalization.[2] By the end of the story it is we who now see the horror of the event.

The character of Ken Smythe, the public relations man for the Essen International Amity Boys Brass Band, suggests that one of the reasons for a division between the artist and his audience is the unwarranted intervention of such mediating figures. In an analogy to literature, Smythe might correspond to the publisher, editor, bookseller, or the critic. He is completely ignorant about both the compositions the band has chosen to play and the quality of their performing art. As the program continues, he proceeds to get drunk and, in so doing, increasingly reveals his racism and his lower-class, boorish values. Despite the veneer of middle-class manners, his voice reveals itself as working-class. This disparity is suggested, first of all, in the metonymic details of his appearance that have causal overtones in that they are character traits over which he has control and in our first glimpse of his behavior:

A man in a blue blazer and grey flannels came on and lowered the microphone. One of the two men who had been setting out the chairs spoke to him as they were leaving the stage.
"What, mate?" boomed over the sound-system as the blazer man turned in answer.

There was a brightly coloured badge on the breast pocket. The blazer
man nodded and then turned back tapping the microphone head and
blowing into it. He cleared his throat.

"Good evening . . . " he began, but then waited as people edged
along the wooden rows back to their seats. His sleek hair gleamed in the
lights. (*TMF*, 11–12)

Notice the sense of unprofessionalism, the betrayal of the lower class
in the idiom "mate," the pejorative connotations in the carefully
chosen adjective "sleek," and the glossy, artificial suggestions in
the entire remark, "His sleek hair gleamed in the lights."

The discrepancy in Smythe's character is also suggested in the
ironic dimensions of the title of the story—the pretentiousness in
the name "Smythe" instead of "Smith," the disparity in the juxtaposition of the informal "Ken" where one would expect "Kenneth," and the fundamental irony of "strange" and the ironic
pomposity of "aberration" in that we ultimately learn that his vulgar
behavior is not strange at all and certainly not an aberration. It is
merely his normal nature manifesting itself. Smythe is really responsible for the chaos and horror that we witness, but the story
makes clear that it is necessary to perform the craft in spite of such
false mediators.

It is necessary to perform the craft in spite of other obstacles too.
Metcalf spends considerable space, as he establishes firmly the focus
of the traveler, detailing the time and the physical and social characteristics of the environment in which the municipal entertainments
will take place because the details are metonymic signifiers for the
vulgarity of the artistic tastes and sensibilities of the audience for
which the band must perform. The story begins with a fading vision
of a romantic ideal, represented by Edinburgh Castle, and with a
literal and metaphorical descent into darkness (*TMF*, 7–8). The
startling shout and the football crashing through the trees are just
two of the details in the initial scene that metaphorically anticipate
the frenzied havoc that will ensue during the performance of the
band (*TMF*, 8).

The first performance that we witness is that of the Glasgow
Variety Show to which we are introduced by a second-rate master
of ceremonies comedian who indulges in cheap scatological humor
and whose initial remark, although uttered in jest, ironically foreshadows the real hostility that will emerge later:

. . . As the piper finished, a short, fat man in evening dress bustled out trailing the cord of a hand-mike. He bowed to the piper and then held up his hand for silence.

"You're hostile before we've even started, aren't you?" . . . (*TMF* 9)

Metcalf uses the Glasgow Variety Show for juxtaposed comic effects. To begin with, it is a low vulgar form of art, the sort of acts that one might have seen on the Ed Sullivan Show or in vaudeville theater:

"And now," said the short, fat man, "now, it is an honour to present those two great stars of our own National Opera Company, the ever-young, the ever-popular, those dearly loved . . . "

"Get ON with it," bawled a voice from the darkness.

"Thank you," said the short, fat man bowing and smiling.

"Ladies and gentlemen," he continued, "those luminaries, Scotland's best loved soprano voice—Miss Helen Foster and . . ."

Wailing nearer and nearer along Princes Street the siren of an ambulance or police car.

"And here she comes now!" cried the short, fat man flinging out his arm towards the pulsating sound. "Always practising!"

He giggled and held up his hand. (*TMF,* 10)

The voice from the darkness, like the MC's remark about hostility, is a prelude to the later active aggression of the audience toward the brass band; and the paragraphed detail about the wailing siren, in its isolation and incongruous juxtaposition, suggests the external interference with which the artist must cope in performing his craft and foreshadows the intense external pressures in spite of which the band must perform.

The art of the Glasgow Variety Show contrasts strikingly with the professional, disciplined, and austere performance of the brass band, qualities that Metcalf initially suggests in the stylistic and grammatical precision of the first sentences he uses to describe the band's opening selection:

. . . Suddenly onto the stage strode a man in a black suit, halted, faced the silent band. The arm of Herr Kunst rose; the arm of Herr Kunst descended.

The burst of sound was crisp and perfect, the sections rising and sitting as one man, the soloist flawless. Herr Kunst stood rigid except for the metronome pump of his elbows. (*TMF,* 13)

"Kunst," of course, means in German "art," and, together with Fraulein Christina Hohenstaufen and Heine, he is the principal representative of the artist in the story. Like "Kunst," Christina Hohenstaufen is a name with analogical significance, her first name obviously associating her typologically with Christ as victim and her second name associating her with nobility.

The response to the Glasgow Variety Show is enthusiastic, a response that ironically suggests the limited tastes of the audience and thus intensifies the anxiety about the brass band's performance for such an audience. But the restiveness of the audience before and during the performance suggests an uneasiness about art in general, and there is also the strong suggestion that the positive response occurs not solely or even primarily as a response to the art of the performers as art but because the performers are Scottish. Through the juxtaposition of two traditionally antagonistic national labels on that art, Metcalf is subtly suggesting by the differentiated response to the two performances that art as art should transcend national boundaries. That the audience, with the help of Ken Smythe, is actively hostile to the high and responsive to the low suggests that nationalism and racism distort an appreciation of art and that the burden of communication does not rest solely with the artist. The audience is the producer of meaning, and it must educate itself. Metcalf deliberately intensifies the strain for a pure aesthetic response by conjuring up the morally repugnant associations of Nazism and the Hitler youth movement in his descriptions of the military appearance and behavior of Herr Kunst and the band.

Metcalf, throughout all his stories, frequently uses the paragraph as a rhetorical device to emphasize the importance of a detail or an image by the implied status in the isolating effect, an effect that he often uses for ironic purposes. The sinister nature of the meaning of the restive crowd is emphasized, for example, in the following one-sentence paragraph:

On the grass below the stage, a confusion of dark figures marched. (*TMF*, 20)

The symbolic dissolution of Fraulein Hohenstaufen and her diminished strength in contrast to Herr Kunst as she begins to yield to the pressure of the mob are suggested in the following paragraph:

A long wisp of hair had worked loose from the Fraulein's coiled braids. Her fingers tried to brush it from her face and tuck it behind her ear. She half-turned for a moment to glance at Herr Kunst's back. (*TMF*, 19)

As the story moves toward its climax, as the crowd becomes increasingly frenzied, the rhythm of the sentences and the intensity of the language, as well as the paragraphing, all convey the rising emotional crescendo of the moment only to end with the deflating, abrupt, and emotionally staggering attack on the artist (*TMF*, 20–21). Not to mention the fact that it is the chauvinistic *Colonel Bogey* march that the band is playing, the power and emotional efficacy of the band's performance itself contributes paradoxically to the attack upon the artist.

Throughout the entire event, Metcalf has interspersed at strategic points details of the American family who are behaving as if they were at Yankee Stadium and filming the event on their camera, and he ends with the total moral and emotional disparity of their response and with the greater horror of their recording the horror of the assault.[3] They are just as guilty as the mob, if not more so, not only because they are implicitly part of the mob, but also because they wish to record and preserve the moral outrage. Perhaps we are all culpable, even the traveler, who "joined the queue of children and mothers and bought a sixpenny cone" (*TMF*, 8).

The second story in the sequence, "The Practice of the Craft," deals openly with the tension between the artist's professional and personal life. It is the story of a professional actor who is playing the lead role in a West End farce about a man whose young wife is unfaithful to him and which actor, as we gradually learn through carefully placed expository details throughout the story, is suffering the same fate in his own personal life as the character whom he portrays in the play. The rhetorical thrust of the story suggests that in order to practice his craft it might be necessary for the artist to sacrifice the personal reality of his own life for the sake of the craft itself. The excruciating agony of this dilemma is emphasized by the ironic parallel between the actor's personal situation and the plot of the play: every night in a small provincial theater he acts out a farce of the tragedy of his own life; and he will continue, must continue, to perform this ritualistic masochism simply because he is a professional actor and because his pain is the price that he must pay for what he is.

The suffering of his situation is intensified simply because of his awareness of the parallel between himself and the character he plays. The tension between his professional and personal life would have still existed had he been playing any other role, but that he must play himself doubles the ironic pressure. Two other factors contribute significantly to this irony. Although the actor is a thoroughly professional and dedicated craftsman, he is not really a star, and he is not practicing his craft, say, on Broadway or in Hollywood. The fame and monetary rewards resulting from such a situation would have extenuated the irony of his circumstances, would have made his decision to sacrifice his personal life more understandable and acceptable, but Metcalf obviates such a possibility by focusing on a pure dedication to the craft itself, however dubious the rewards of that dedication are. That the actor knows that the play itself is second-rate drama and that his part in it is less than demanding on his talents compounds the irony and stresses his professionalism, for, despite these inadequacies, he will do a thoroughly professional job.

The point of view is a third-person center of consciousness for the most part, but the effaced narrator appears once in a while to give us narrative summaries, as in the opening expository paragraph, a very unusual beginning for Metcalf (*TMF, 46*). Metcalf communicates the want-ought nature of the actor's predicament in several ways. He is continually juxtaposing descriptive details about the actor's professional, disciplined habits[4] with glimpses into the actor's mind that reveal the anxiety of his personal life, and the effect is twofold—both irony and a heightened emotional contrast. The indecorum of the contiguous details stresses their difference and intensifies the emotional impact of their juxtaposition (*TMF, 54– 56*). Metcalf also uses typography to stress the diametric dimensions of the actor's condition. In the following passage "Luck Love Janet" and the code on the telegram are both printed in full capitals and indented paragraphs:

The message on the telegram read:
LUCK LOVE JANET
The stage manager's voice cut in over the house music and the noise of the audience.
*Five minutes. Five minutes, please.*

Neil Peters found himself reading the mysterious code on the telegram form.

ECB 140 (141140)
TNV 246 CRT TORONTO 9 941P EDT. (*TMF*, 46–47)

By inviting a visual identification between the two groups of words, Metcalf is implying that they should be equated in other ways: both are indecipherable, inscrutable; both are painfully perplexing; both are meaningless.

Two central images in the story crystallize the actor's dilemma: his response to a child of a fellow actor, which is both a reminder of his anguish and a concrete vision of the way in which his professional and personal life could be feasibly reconciled, and the recurring anxiety dream of the log boom, a grotesque image of disintegration that suggests a self-destructive urge and represents an anticipated failure should he reveal his true feelings to his wife (*TMF*, 50; 52–53). Later, in his dressing room, the image of the log boom recurs, suggesting in its tone and precise adjectives, however, an acceptance of the way things really are and the way they must be:

He went back into the dressing room and sipping the bitter coffee, stared at his face. Not a face from Edvard Munch. Quite the wrong image. Dreams distorted things. No desperate clinging. The logs would part, would ride together again, smooth acceptance into the brown world of the river. (*TMF*, 53)

His reading of Neville Chamberlain's biography and his acceptance of the role of Willy Loman in Montreal complement this sense of acceptance.

Such a story might generate an unwarranted sentimentality, but Metcalf mitigates the possibility of excessive pathos by allowing the actor, in four one-sentence paragraphs that dramatize the nature of his predicament through antithetical juxtaposition, to accept his pain and mock it simultaneously:

. . . He wiped the counter clean and then looked at himself in the mirror.
Iago to his own Othello?
He shrugged the jacket to settle it comfortably.
Her last consort had even left a toothbrush.
He bowed to his reflection. (*TMF*, 56)

Through his ironic bow to himself in the bright lights of the dressing room mirror, a physical gesture that is a ritual of his profession, he exhibits an emotional acceptance of both the mutilation of his feelings imposed upon him by his wife's behavior and the pain of the discipline imposed upon him by himself to parody himself. The distancing effect is necessary here, for it not only reduces the sentimentality for the reader, but also tempers the self-pity of the actor. The self-mockery, moreover, as well as the actor's sympathy for Katie, a young technical assistant who has given up everything to be part of the theatrical company, indicates that, unlike the situation in "The Strange Aberration of Mr. Ken Smythe," Metcalf is aware of the fundamental irony of the artist's choice to be an artist. By definition, he must be separated from his community, but that is a conscious choice. But there is also the subtle suggestion of an active rather than a passive stance at the very end of the story in that, in terms of the parallel between the character he plays and his own personal life, Neil Peters may confront his wife directly with her infidelity. The following lines of the part of the script of the play we are given are added to the earlier version we have already read:

EDWARD: And once the week before that. That was a dress-fitting, wasn't it? Or was it curtains? I seem to remember something about curtains.

LAVINIA: Curtains. You remember. For the dining room.

*He sets his drink down and faces her.*

EDWARD: Lavinia?

LAVINIA: Umm?

EDWARD: Who is he, darling? (*TMF,* 57)

As in "The Strange Aberration of Mr. Ken Smythe," there is a prominent satiric strain in "Gentle as Flowers Make the Stones"— ridicule of real estate agencies, hippies, nature-organic freaks, women's liberation, pseudopoets, pseudonovelists, avante-garde literary magazines, book review editors, *Reader's Digest,* booksellers, the Canadian Author's Association, academe, suburbia, and the Jewish nouveau riche.[5] The satire, however, is not mere invective self-indulgence. The attitudes of ridicule are a device of characterization, for we see everything through the eyes of a poet named Jim Haine who lives purely and simply for the art that he practices. Despite the exigencies of his life—his need for money, food (he keeps his "completed poems and worksheets" in the fridge and only scraps of food), shelter, human companionship, even the necessity to defecate—he must practice his craft. In a washroom of the *Montreal Herald* in four one-sentence paragraphs:

> He lowered his trousers and sat.
> He needed money.
> He needed breakfast.
> He needed a place to live. (*TMF*, 29)

And later in two one-sentence paragraphs:

> He strained and grunted.
> *veteres patronos.* (*TMF*, 30)

And still later in a restaurant: "He found that he was gazing at the cinnamon Danish; he wanted the cinnamon Danish very much. He could feel the pressure of the final stanza, the bulge and push of it in his head. The hunger had turned to hollow pain" (*TMF*, 35). Not hesitating to compromise himself morally for his craft, he consistently uses people and is even willing to sell drugs for the money to survive and to practice his art. Throughout the story Haine is composing a poem in his mind, a translation of one of Martial's epigrams that is an elegy for a dead child. The completion of the poem, which is the climax of the story, occurs during a moment of sexual climax with a woman who is presumably emotionally and sexually starved for him. Yet while the entire sexual encounter is taking place, all that is going on in his mind is the birth of the poem that he has been working on all day.

The story suggests that to be an artist is to be utterly cut off from life and all genuine human contact, but it also raises the issue of whether the artist's isolation is self-imposed and what his motives are in choosing to be an artist. The classical, Jonsonian precision of the poem that the poet finally creates is in stark contrast to the chaos and fragmentation of his life—not unlike the contrast between the art represented by the Essen Amity Boys Brass Band and the context in which they perform. In this contrast and in the poet's obvious joy in creativity lies a strong implication that art is superior to life and that the isolation of the artist is self-willed. The satiric attitudes thus indicate the poet's sense of superiority and self-distancing from the world. Metcalf confirms this stance by revealing at strategic points throughout the story that intensify the dialectic between art and life that the poet is divorced and making child-support payments. In the context of these expository details the elegy that the poet is translating thus becomes a paradoxical lament for his own lost child and the normal personal life that he has given up to practice his craft—a lament, in other words, for the loss of life itself. The artist has sealed himself away from the world because of the demands of his art.

The poet's compulsion to lie about his occupation emphasizes his sense of vulnerability, his isolation, and his implicit awareness that his profession is unacceptable to society. Any of the tenuously acceptable professions that Haine claims to be his own—"a professor at McGill, a male nurse, a pest-control officer, a journalist" (*TMF*, 27)—would be considered more respectable than the profession of poet, and so as poet he withdraws from the world. The initial paragraphs of the story, an in-medias-res beginning of scenic report, also lead us to an awareness of the nakedness of the artist, stripped of the vestments of normal social existence, persistently attempting to spawn new art despite frustrating odds:

Fists, teeth clenched, Jim Haine stood naked and shivering staring at the lighted rectangle. He must have slept through the first knocks, the calling. Even the buzzing of the doorbell had made them nervous; he'd had to wad it up with paper days before. The pounding and shouting continued. The male was beginning to dart through the trails between the *Aponogeton crispus* and the blades of the *Echinodorus martii*.

Above the pounding, words: 'passkey,' 'furniture,' 'bailiffs.'
............................................................

The female was losing colour rapidly. She'd shaken off the feeding fry and was diving and pancaking through the weed-trails.

Hour after hour he had watched the two fish cleaning one of the blades of a Sword plant, watched their ritual procession, watched the female dotting the pearly eggs in rows up the length of the leaf, the milt-shedding male following; slow, solemn, seeming to move without motion, like carved galleons or bright painted rocking-horses.

The first eggs had turned grey, broken down to flocculent slime; the second hatch, despite copper sulphate and the addition of peat extracts, had simply died.

"I know you're in there, Mr. Haine!"
A renewed burst of door-knob rattling.
He had watched the parents fanning the eggs; watched them stand guard. Nightly, during the hatch, he had watched the parents transport the jelly blobs to new hiding places, watched them spitting the blobs onto the underside of leaves to hang glued and wriggling. He had watched the fry become free-swimming, discover the flat sides of their parents, wriggle and feed there from the mucous secretions.
"Tomorrow . . . hands of our lawyers!"
The shouting and vibration stopped too late.
The frenzied Discus had turned on the fry, snapping, engulfing, beaking through their brood. (*TMF,* 22–23)[6]

But as Haine stands listening to the assault upon his door, he sees the parent fish, frenzied by the unnatural noise and vibration, turn and devour their own brood. "He didn't stay to watch the carnage; the flash of the turning fish, the litter floating across the surface of the tank, the tiny commas drifting towards the suction of the filter's mouth" (*TMF,* 23).

The painstaking and delicate generative activity of the fish is a metonym metaphorically signifying the poetic process, and the parents' devouring of their own brood is a metonym metaphorically signifying how art may, in the face of frustrating odds, occasionally destroy itself. But there is an irony in this awareness, for Haine has tried to breed the fish only for money to survive in order to practice his craft (*TMF,* 25).

Even more compelling is the final scene, in which Metcalf, through a startling juxtaposition of the events that are literally taking place and the literal events in the poet's head, dramatizes with a simultaneously pathetic and bitter irony the exact nature of the poet's plight (*TMF,* 44–45). The total failure in verbal and emotional communication, the joy of the poet's creative climax and the a-generative birth of his poem in contrast to the nongenerative sexual encounter and joyless sexual climax, and merely the fact that the attempt at human contact here is on a sloppy, vulgar level in the back seat of a car—it is not even intercourse—all intensify the ironic pathos of the incident. It seems indeed significant that the sexual gratification is not simultaneous and that the fellatio is not a complete act. In terms of the theme of poetic creativity and the odds against which it must take place as well as the sexual and ironic generative dimensions of this scene, the entire episode should also be compared with the generative activity of the fish, the image that initiates the story. Notice, for example, merely the connection between the description of the fish as "commas" and the poet's discovery that commas are his "balancing pole" (*TMF*, 45). The intense irony of this ending is a rhetorical heightening that functions as a story-closing signal reducing the effect of openness.

Metcalf's use of a first-person point of view in the final two stories of the sequence indicates that the problem of the artist's predicament that he is exploring in these five stories has become more internal and particularized. Although the novelist of "The Years in Exile," for example, is not Metcalf, he might be considered a symbolic surrogate for the author. His aesthetics are strikingly similar to Metcalf's own:

> I have always disliked Wordsworth. Once, I must admit, I thought I disliked him for his bathos, his lugubrious tone. But now, I know that it is because he could not do justice to the truth; no philosophical cast of mind can do justice to particularity.
> I am uncomfortable with abstraction, his or mine. (*TMF*, 88–89)

> What will the young man say to me this evening? And what can I say to him? It is difficult to talk to these young college men whose minds no longer move in pictures. Had he been here this morning I could, like some Zen sage, have pointed to the Monarchs about the apple leaves and preserved my silence.
> Particular life. Particular life.
> All else is tricks of the trade or inexpressible. (*TMF*, 98)

The first-person point of view, however, in which the narrator is both internal focalizer and focalized, also reminds us of the problematic use of the pronoun "I" in any discourse. The "I" speaking and the "I" spoken about can never be the same, and neither of these is the extratextual, empirical "I" which hovers, as Italo Calvino says, at the shoulder of the "I" who is speaking.[7] The "I" in the narrated event, the subject of the enounced, in other words, is always sliding away from the "I" doing the speaking, the subject of the speaking event, the enunciation. Within the fiction of "The Years in Exile" the novelist is the enunciating agent speaking about a character called "I" or "myself" from somewhere else, and especially in those portions of the story that are retrospective there is, as in third person, a division between narration and focus. When we read the story, however, thus becoming enunciating agents, the producers of meaning, ourselves, we become the "I."

The story focuses on the inherent psychic split in the novelist's mind simply because he is a novelist. Because he has fictionalized the past, because he has framed "its insistence" through the internal fictionalizing process of memory, the novelist's visions of his childhood at the age of nine or ten are more real to him than his present moment in Canada as a famous novelist. The fictionalizing operation of memory, as the novelist himself knows, is "the most basic form of creativity" (*TMF*, 99). Memory, like fiction, edits, orders, and preserves (produces) experience. Memory, like language its medium, shapes, produces, invents experience, giving it meaning, and ultimately yields through it mythologizing effects a sense of identity, the supreme fiction. The narrative structures or informing myths of fiction are not merely recurring structures of novels and short stories, but also constructs of the human imagination and memory whose medium is language. Through language, we imagine everything and everyone, we invent everything and everyone, we remember everything and everyone—including ourselves. Insofar as experience is available for comment, insofar as it has meaning, insofar as it is present to us— immediately in front of us now—it is available only as fiction: *fingere* (to shape or to make).

Home is a psychic state of oneness, of identity, in which one's world is not an external environment but part of one. Consequently, the novelist's memories of his childhood past in England, because he has mythologized the past, are his internal home:

Many might dismiss such meaningless particulars of memory.
I know that I am lost in silence hours on end dwelling on another time now more real to me than this chair, more real than the sunshine filtering through the fawn and green of the willow tree. (*TMF*, 82)

Identifying himself with Wilcher in Joyce Cary's *To Be a Pilgrim,* he thinks:

Yes, I have thought myself a pilgrim, the books my milestones. But these recent weeks, the images that haunt my nights and days . . .
I have seen the holy places though I never knew it. I have travelled on, not knowing all my life that the mecca of my pilgrimage had been reached so young, and that all after was the homeward journey. (*TMF*, 83)

Because the novelist's real home lies in his visions of the past, his present moment becomes, as the title of the story implies, a metaphorical condition of exile and expatriation.

The detailed vividness and immediacy of the many passages that focus on the past throughout the story both illustrate the novelist's (and Metcalf's) aesthetic about particularity and convey the reality of the novelist's visions. He can smell the honeysuckle and feel the magistrate's ledger, which as a young boy he once found in a spoiled mansion, Fortnell House, which has its analogy in Wilcher's Tolbrook; he thinks "more often, and with greater bitterness," of the two willow-pattern plates that he stole from the house than he does of his first wife; and the body of Patricia Hopkins, who gave him a glimpse of "the smooth cleft mound of her vagina" (*TMF*, 99) at the age of nine is "better remembered than the bodies of two wives" (*TMF*, 99). All of the descriptive passages of his past experiences are really metonyms metaphorically signifying the novelist's psychic condition of being at home.

The past-present, fiction-life opposition that Metcalf is exploring in this story parallels the other antitheses in his fiction referred to earlier. In "The Years in Exile" he specifically identifies the particularity and vividness of the past with nature. The color of the petunias, the willows (associated with the willow-pattern plates that comforted him through the years), the Monarch butterflies—all objects of the novelist's perception in the present moment—for example, are associated with the reality of the details perceived through memory. The story begins significantly with an immediate juxtaposition of the past and the present, the pastoral and the urban, and the natural and the synthetic along with a sense of the novelist's discomfort and alienation in the present moment (*TMF*, 80).

One of the ways in which Metcalf stresses the reality of the novelist's fictionalized dreams of his past is by associating the state of the old man's physical decay with the decay of the eighteenth-century manor house, Fortnell House, which is the focal point of his reveries. The house itself stands for the vitiation of English society, manners, and values. Despite their physical decomposition, however, both the novelist and the house are alive in a more vital way through the fictionalizing activity of the novelist. The old man's movement around the lawn throughout the story in order to remain in the sunlight suggests this vitality and his desire or need to persist in the "life" of his reveries, and the story ends with the image specifically associated with his past. Although the sun has literally "long since passed over the house," he remains in the sunlight of his dreams: " . . . I should go and shave. But I will sit a little longer in the sunshine. Here between the moored houseboats where I can watch the turn of the quicksilver dace. Here by the piles of the bridge where in the refracted sunlight swim the golden-barred and red-finned perch" (*TMF*, 101).

The stories that I have dealt with thus far have examined hypothetically through pure fictional figures the plight of the artist in general. "The Teeth of My Father" deals not only with the general problem of the relation between life and art, but also with the relationship between Metcalf's own empirical life and his own art, short story writing. Specifically, it explores the truth of fiction as opposed to the putative factual truth of life, but it is also a moving elegy for Metcalf's father and a summing-up of his rhetorical concerns as a writer.

Early in the story, which incorporates whole stories and parts of others that Metcalf has previously written, the fictional enunciating "I" utters a remark that is both an admonition to and a directive for the readers: "(I have decided to tell the truth. My stories in the River Room were not purely nostalgic; they were calculated to be funny and entertain my friend. My friend was more an acquaintance, a man I admired and wanted to impress. And 'wilful legs' was plagiarized from Dylan Thomas.)" (*TMF*, 59)

The effect of this remark is multiple. It complicates an already problematic relationship between the "I" of the enunciation and the "I" of the enounced. It shatters the art illusion of the main level of narration up to this point, raising the level of narration to another level which now becomes the main one as the original level becomes a second degree of narration even as the incorporation of other Metcalf stories and parts of stories represent a third degree. In other words, the shattering of the art illusion of classical realism is itself another art illusion. It also establishes the fictional structure of the story as an autobiographical one; it draws attention to the fact that the story is indeed fiction and to the writer's performance as fiction writer; and, finally, it invites the reader to realize that whether the incidents about to be narrated concerning the relationship between father and son are inventive or factual is irrelevant. The story, because it is fiction, a distillation of experience, which is available to us only through language anyway, has an imaginative truth that is more real, more true emotionally and psychologically, than autobiography in any factual or historical sense. All autobiography is, in fact, fiction. The story appears to be—indeed, admits to be through the speaking voice of the "I"—the "truth," but it is a truth that is a supreme piece of fiction. "The Teeth of My Father," then, is really about the craft of fiction itself, about the writer's art of shaping or manipulating empirical experience to give it a greater reality, about language.

Breaking from one level of text to another can undermine the credibility of the text and the reliability of the narrator. Why should we believe the new narrator any more than the first? But in any case it draws attention to the problematic nature of truth, to the status of the text as fiction, and to the art of fiction. Like the directive but not so startlingly, the narrator's introductions to the incorporated stories serve these functions, though an even more obvious instance is the two voices—one in italics, the invented voice of a critic (which pushes the level of the incorporated stories down to a fourth degree of narration), and one in ordinary type, the speaking "I"—of the metanarrative comments immediately after the presentation of the story "Biscuits":

> *It is instructive, ladies and gentlemen, to examine the psychological implications of this sample of juvenilia if we may assume it to be autobiographical either in fact or impulse.*
> Yes, you can assume that.
> *What activity is the child essentially engaged in? In nothing more or less than the act of defining his identity. Through which functions does the child perform this act? Through naming, drawing, and most importantly, writing. And with which parent does this suggest identification?*
> *Exactly so. Exactly so. The father!*
> *Who, who I may remind you is, in the words of the text, 'far away.' For the perceptive reader, the point requires no further elucidation.* (TMF, 63)

The incorporation of other Metcalf stories into "The Teeth of My Father" has several effects. All the stories have an autobiographical fictional structure, and so we have autobiography within autobiography, fiction within fiction; and despite the reader's factual knowledge that Metcalf did indeed write these stories, there is the added fiction that the persona, the "I", of "The Teeth of My Father" is the author of the stories. Is "The Teeth of My Father" "*autobio-*

*graphical either in fact or impulse"? "For the perceptive reader, the point
requires no further elucidation" (TMF, 63).*

Many of the incidents here related no doubt are pure invention—
the loose-box incident, for example. Many are edited facts—Metcalf's father did not make a new pair of teeth every week. But all
are true emotionally and psychologically, more illustrative of the
way the father really was from the narrator's point of view than any
factual truth. The story ends with an apostrophe, an elegiac lament
of an "I" that is, if not John Metcalf in empirical fact, then John
Metcalf in truth:

> I did not cry.
> On the evening I received news of your death I went to the Esquire
> Show Bar on Stanley Street in Montreal and listened to King Curtis leading
> a blues band.
> I did not cry.
> I was irritated at your funeral by the tear-sodden faces and the predictable
> rhetoric of the officiating minister. Looking at your coffin, I was not
> moved. My thoughts were of the borrowed airfare, the yellowed soles of
> your feet, toenails.
> I was not moved to tears.
> Yet I did go into your study which still stank of your tobacco and I
> took your red propelling-pencil and your fountain pen.
> Now, ten years later in a life half done, a life distinctly lacking in
> probity, I use your pen, now twice-repaired, to write my stories, your
> pencil for corrections.
> And I am crying now.
> Drunken tears but tears for you. For you. For both of us. Standing on
> the sidewalk in the cold fall evening of another country my tears are
> scalding. (TMF, 79).

Notice the weights and emphases created by the paragraphing here,
especially the emotional rising in the polyptotonic repetition of the
notion of crying/tears.

Metcalf has only a few interrogative texts, as Catherine Belsey
would call them,[8] that show such fabulation impulses so overtly—
that is, the inclusion in fiction of further fictions imagined by
fictional characters or presented by the narrator himself as alternative
versions of events—but the effect is very much like a Brechtian
alienation effect: an implicit repudiation of the illusionism of bourgeois realism. It questions the assumption that fiction directly re-

produces the world, and it makes us not passive consumers of "works" but coproducers of "texts." In questioning the borderline between reality and fiction and emphasizing metafictionally the status of the text as artifact, the story implies that there is nothing but fiction, no reality apart from its narration, no being except through language. We are reminded that we are not really watching life but reading fiction, that fiction is language, that stories and people in fiction are merely words, and that there are really no descriptions in fiction, only constructions.

# Chapter Five
# Novellas

Genre may be thought of as a set of norms, a set of expectations that structure our reading of texts, allowing us to organize our experience and understanding of the text according to conventional patterns and to recognize variations in the use of conventions. But for Metcalf, the novella is not really a form of discourse or genre radically distinct from the short story, for the impulse of both is poetic. The imagistic, metonymic patterns, the texture, and the plot are not inherently more complex than they would be in a short story but merely extended or amplified, making the narrative weightier and giving it a certain magnitude. Short stories compress, novels expand, but novellas do both. Novellas allow for both intensity and expansion through a network of motifs that intensifies the treatment of the subject and through a structure of insistent repetition that simultaneously permits the development of parallel situations and exposes that network of motifs in various contexts. In brief, the novella is, as E. D. Blodgett has put it so aptly, "a dialectical transformation of techniques appropriate to both the short story and the novel."[1]

Yet length is not a completely irrelevant factor when a novella and a short story are compared in terms of reader response. There are experiential differences in pace, in duration, in the extent of our expectations and revisions as we read, and usually in the degree of inferentiality required by the story inscribed in the text. In other words, the novella is a different narrative from a short story, not because of what it is but because, as Jerome Beaty points out,[2] of what we in a sense become while we read. In any case, because the narrative does not have to be as tight, a novella's medial scope provides an effective range to render the "degenerative" or "pathetic" kind of tragedy, as Mary Doyle Springer calls it,[3] in which the protagonist's fate is neither heroic nor trivial—an apposite description of all three of Metcalf's novellas.

## *The Lady Who Sold Furniture*

Like Metcalf's other novellas, *The Lady Who Sold Furniture,* rendered through a third-person center of consciousness, is divided into chapters or sections—in this case, four—a form of punctuation appropriate to the novella that controls the pace of our reading, inviting us to recapitulate what has happened and to project what might come. The thematic pulse of this story is the ambiguous nature of the relationship between Peter Hendricks, a recent university graduate about to launch a teaching career at a British secondary comprehensive school, and his older lover, Jeanne, the housekeeper in his old boarding house to which he has returned after a summer's work. What Peter learns is that Jeanne is the lady who sold furniture of the title—but it is other people's furniture.

The story is very Caryesque in its mixture of the humorous and pathetic, but especially in its exploration of the moral conflict between the variation on Cary's creative individual represented by Jeanne and the variation on Cary's conservative man represented by Peter.[4] Like Dick Bowser, Charley Brown, and Mr. Johnson, Jeanne is an artist without a medium, an anarchist ignoring all claims but her own; having been institutionalized once, now committed to freedom; and invariably in conflict with authority because the displaced form her art takes is crime. She is, in Cary's terms, an artist in life itself, for to Cary to be alive is to be in a state of continuous creation. Conservative man, on the other hand, is bound to the past and must do battle with the impulse to create within himself. Notice, for example, the large expository chunks of flashback in the first part of section one and the unusual sense of nostalgia for not a distant but a recent past (*LSF,* 7–9), Peter's awareness of the pastness of the past. These memories provide an anterior expository report, but they also characterize Peter. His metonymic association with order, discipline, responsibility, cleanliness, a structured society, and images of time, however, implicitly repudiate his past creative, festive life, a life qualitatively associated with Jeanne. Consider his implicitly elegiac remembrance of the incomplete collection of football cards and the comic serial he never completed—not to mention the obvious significance of his cleaning and washing on the morning after the final party at the Compton-Smythes (*LSF,* 95).

Jeanne, in contrast, is identified with metonymic details of disorder, partying, freedom, with a natural or pastoral environment, with a lack of concern about time and the past, and with a fluid identity (Mrs. Beazley, Anderson, or Carlyle). The garbled allusion made by Jim, the landlord, to Prince Hal in *1 Henry IV* alerts us not only to the analogy between Hal and Peter in their respective repudiations of their past sporting lives and their embracing of present responsibility, but also to the notion of Falstaffian "holiday" and disregard for time associated with Jeanne. (See the famous speeches by Hal at I.2.2–12 and I.2.199–200.) This Falstaffian holiday motif is reinforced by the abundance of drinking and meal scenes with Jeanne and by the explicit references to holidays after each of the two thefts of furniture (*LSF*, 35, 93), once by Jeanne and once by her daughter, Anna.

Peter, again in contrast to Jeanne, is associated on several occasions with time and specifically with clocks (*LSF*, 57, 62, 64, 71, 72, 80, 84). The scene in the pub waiting and watching for the bus and overhearing the two old men, a reworking of an early story, "Just Two Old Men,"[5] reiterates the time motif and an awareness of the pastness of the past, as does the conversation with Henry about his old auntie and all the references by Mr. Arckle to furniture of the past, a past of which Jeanne is quite willing to be rid. Consider the reference to her story of smuggling watches (*LSF*, 25) and her singling out of the grandfather clock to be taken during the second theft (*LSF*, 101). Mr. Arckle's response to her about the clock is suggestively Falstaffian: "That's no good to us" (*LSF*, 101).

But it is not a black-and-white antithesis between Jeanne and Peter. She weeps on her forty-third birthday, an act indicating her awareness of time and the pastness of the past, and she claims she's too old to eat cucumbers (*LSF*, 46). On two occasions, moreover, despite her willingness to indulge in grand theft, she displays an ironic moral concern about Anna's possible discovery of Peter in her bed (*LSF*, 56, 89). Then, too, although she is associated with the natural, the pastoral, the festive—on their first night together (reported through flashback), for example, she picks an armful of lilac branches—she is ambiguously associated with night and dark or black colors (*LSF*, 10, 79, 80). Peter's choice is no norm either as we learn through his perceptions and apperceptions of Gartree and Gartree Comprehensive School. Here is part of his first experience of Gartree:

Peter looked out of the window at the parallel rows of streets. The concrete council houses marched along each road and out of sight as the bus passed. Hazel Row. Blackthorn Street. Honeysuckle Drive. Elderberry Avenue. Briar Street. There was not a tree in sight.

The bus stopped and he got out and looked around the Square. There were shops on all four sides and, in the centre, a public lavatory. . . .

The school was glass and coloured panels, a deserted stretch of asphalt, ragged shrubs in a strip of garden by the front doors. It had taken him half an hour from the city centre. He stared through the railings.

On the padlocked gates was a metal shield—a blue ground on which was painted an oak tree. . . .

He turned back towards Gartree Square. He cut through Magnolia Street and passed a small public garden which was surrounded by a wire-mesh fence. An old man in a black overcoat was sitting on a concrete bench staring at the floral clock. (*LSF,* 17–18)

Notice the metonymic significance of the irony of the names of the streets, the presence of only ragged shrubs and no trees, the artificial militaristic order, the images of enclosure—the Square, the pad locked gates, the railings, the wire-mesh fence—and the old man staring at the floral clock. Time is a social convention by which the flux of life is made measurable by imposing patterns on it—by machines such as clocks, watches, calendars, for instance. But time is also, paradoxically, repetition within irreversible change. It is to this life that Peter has committed himself, a world preoccupied with and structured by time and all its metonyms.

On his first day of classes, in immediate contrast to the disordered quarters of his friend, Allan, where he is staying (*LSF,* 61), he enters the following enclosed ersatz world of forms, regulations, "enamel flowers," and pastoral reproductions: "The glass doors of the foyer sighed shut behind him, cutting off the surge and babble of the playground. On the wall facing him was a reproduction of some dim pastoral scene and flanking him two broad-leaved plants in wooden tubs" (*LSF,* 57). Such metonymic details are complemented by the snatches of dialogue overheard in the staff room, the virtual speech of the teachers in Peter's mind, the descriptive details of the staff room and his classroom, and the lack of quality in his students' essays. The absurdity of this world is epitomized in the brilliant caricature of the bizarre headmaster, N. Stine.

Mr. Arckle, the underworld middleman who comes for the furniture, is also a stunning caricature, rendered almost totally through speech, which is in fact foregrounded through the story. There is an abundance of anticipations that subtly prepare us for Arckle's arrival to dismantle the house: Jeanne's theft of the razor blade of Jim (*LSF*, 15) whom, incidentally, she caricatures wonderfully; the remark about Jeanne's smuggling of watches (*LSF*, 25); Jeanne's use of Jim's household money for dinner (*LSF*, 29); the quiet suggestion that her father is a con man of sorts and her remark, also providing a motive for her own behavior, "It's better than being a grocer" (*LSF*, 29–30); the metonymic significance of the description of the empty houses at "the end of the Valley" anticipating metaphorically the "broken," "splintered" dismantling of their relationship (*LSF*, 17); and, of course, most dramatically, the visit of the CID. (*LSF*, 18, 20).

The first time Arckle and his troop arrive to dismantle the house, it is humorous, though the humor is qualified by both the danger and the immorality of the theft. The second time Arckle arrives, it is a metonym metaphorically signifying the dismantling of Peter and Jeanne's relationship, anticipated of course in Arckle's first visit.

Jeanne's gift of the leather document case at the end of the second visit is of ambiguous significance—deliberately so—but there is a strong suggestion, complemented by their earlier discussion of the case, that the gift is a repudiation, a mocking, of his choice to teach and the values it implies. Her actual departure signals closure, but the still shot of his standing in the hall, alone, listening to the sounds of departure emblematizes the mood of the departure. It also implies some efficacy: we sense that there has been some shift in perspective, but we are left uncertain about the nature and extent of any awareness he may have gained.

This strategy of ambiguity in the entire ending is anticipated and complemented by the ambiguity in the discussion they have about freedom and by the possible metonymic significance of the damming of the stream, both of which incidents take place during the pastoral interlude of part 2. As she presses her cigarette coupons into the album, she says,

"You don't get things for free very often in this life" . . .
"They're not *really* free," he said. "You pay for all that with the price of the cigarettes."
"Well they *seem* free, then. Just as important." (*LSF*, 53)

The illusion of freedom—the life she lives as a mediumless artist—
is just as important as a genuine free life. Freedom is an implicit
concept in the dam scene too, and the first thing to notice is the
suspension of time in the scene, metonymically signified by Peter's
stopped watch—stopped by nature, by muddied water. The damming of the stream suggests an attempt to control, to impose upon,
to frustrate nature; but the water trickles through and over, despite
the communal—all three of them participate—effort, and eventually the dam will burst, nature will out. Is this metonymic activity
a metaphoric repudiation of the enclosed, time-bound, artificial,
illusory world Peter has chosen? Is he imposing upon his real festive
nature? There is a strong suggestion that this is so, but there is just
enough ambiguity in the activity to suggest that, paradoxically, the
stream is like time, an irreversible free flow, that the suspension of
time is like the dam, and that the pastoral interlude, like the kestrel
they see, is a rarity, a suspension of the real social world, an illusion
of freedom, even as Jeanne's life is an illusion. And so there is no
easy resolution of the complex dialectic of Jeanne and Peter. Both
live by their illusions despite their implied awareness of those
illusions.

## Girl in Gingham

The point of view in *Girl in Gingham* is a modified third person
in which the focus is internal and the voice is suggestive, for the
most part, of the character focalizer. But the narrator is not always
effaced, and he modulates in and out of the reflector's mind, establishing different levels of voice and of fictional reality. Glimpses
into Peter Thornton's mind are continually being juxtaposed with
dialogue, with metonymic descriptions of external place, time, and
action, and with straightforward narrative exposition. But within
these broad levels are interior sublevels where in fact most of the
action takes place: we experience in Peter's mind conscious thought,
memory, remembered dialogue, imagined dialogue, dream, and
fantasy.

*Girl in Gingham* exhibits some of the persistent binary oppositions
we have seen in Metcalf's other fiction—art and life, fictional and
factual truth, reality and fantasy, comedy and tragedy, humor and
pathos—but the novella specifically revolves around the motive
for—the necessity of and the pain resulting from—"inventing"

people, shaping them to fit the contours of our needs and desires, and "inventing" ourselves or allowing ourselves to be "invented."[6] In terms that the story subtly establishes—Peter persistently sees, or "creates," life in terms of drama, fiction, or painting[7]—it is a story about the necessity to play a role in some play, to be a character in some story, to cast others in roles, to create narrative characters— to shape the play, the story, in order to give life meaning, in order to establish identity. As we move through the story, we learn, through carefully placed flashbacks, glimpses into Peter's mind, and expository details, that his marriage had cast him in the role of husband-father and that with the disintegration of his marriage that role has been stripped completely from him. Divorce takes on a metaphoric dimension.

When we first see Peter, he is suffering the emotional and psychological anguish of a genuine loss of identity, the unbearable reality of which partially accounts for his later tendency to fantasize. There is only tenuous solace in his relationship to the North family, a vicarious experience of his lost family; and he has been reduced to playing the role of "Uncle the Best," a part cast for him by the North's child, Amanda, who is clearly a symbolic substitute for Jeremy, his son: "It was soothing to be with friends in this room with a fire in the fireplace, in this room which was part of a house, part of a household; soothing to be, however briefly, in some sort of context" (*GG*, 91). However precarious, man needs some sense of home, some sense of identity. We also learn that after the breakup of his marriage, Peter's life had become even more structureless when, because of the inadequacies of his roles, he stopped seeing his psychiatrist, whose "office, and he in it . . . was the stuff of comic novels, skits, the weekly fodder of stand-up comedians":

. . . he'd realized that his erstwhile wife, his son, and he, had been reduced to characters in a soap opera which was broadcast every two weeks from Trevore's sound-proofed studio.
And which character was he?
He was the man whom ladies helped in laundromats. He was the man who dined on frozen pies. Whose sink was full of dishes. He was the man in the raincoat who wept in late night bars. (*GG*, 91)

Because he cannot bear the pitiable roles provided by soap opera and low-grade comedy, he remains without a part, characterless.

Consequently, "with a large weariness and a settled habit of sadness," he allows himself to be invented through the ludicrous questionnaire of CompuMate: "Mark the Character Traits which are YOU . . . 'So?' said Alan. 'What would you like to be?' " (GG, 94)

All the details of the first section of the story are important, but the following especially so because they emphatically shape our experience of subsequent sections: 1) Peter's awareness of the absurdity of the modern technological world in which he lives, a situation, like the anguish of his lost self, that partially motivates his romantic fantasies—his attitude toward Dr. Trevore, the "misshapen thing" on Trevore's desk,[8] the "tranquilizing antidepressant psychotherapeutic agents," the toothpicks labeled "Stim-U-Dent: Inter-Dental Stimulators," the "paper plate embossed with the word 'Chi-Net,' " the "straws manufactured by the 'Golden Age Scientific Company,' " and of course the whole phenomenon of CompuMate. 2) The subtle identification— subtle because a commonplace joke— of marriage and death in Alan's remark," . . . you claim you want to get married again. God knows why, but that's *your* funeral," and the idea of death in Amanda's bedtime song, counterpointed by the expository detail that he has tried to commit suicide twice. Both details take on anticipatory significance in view of Anna's death at the end of the story. 3) The memory of the bizarre experience with the "young and beautiful" girl who wanted to share her vision with Peter. The absurdity and the deflating pattern of the experience anticipate the ultimate and absurd destruction of Anna. 4) The final two lines of the section,

He tilted the glass creating changing shapes.
  "I want a girl in gingham,"

establish a quest motif for an ideal and initiate Peter's process of creating that ideal (GG, 97).

One of the ways in which the story is bound together is through the repetition of dinner and drinking scenes. The second section, for example, is set in a restaurant in which we see Peter "creating" his waitress, and it is a scene that metaphorically adumbrates his creation of Anna and the final scene of the story in a restaurant. The waitress is specifically identified with Anna because in both cases the impetus for his creation is the voice of the woman:

It was not the length of leg nor the strange severity of her haircut which attracted him but rather the way she spoke. There was something about her speech; it was nothing as definite as, say, a lisp; if it was an impediment at all it was so slight, so elusive, as to be indefinable. But he was not comfortable with the idea of "impediment"; it did not quite capture what he seemed to hear. That something, he had almost decided, must be the suggestion of a long-ago-lost accent. He found it charming.

He did not know her name.

Sometimes it was Eva. Sometimes Ilse.

. . . . . . . . . . . . . . . . . . . . . . . . . . . . . . . . . . . . . . . . . . . . . . . . . . . . . . . . . . . . . . . . . . . . . .

He watched her deft movements, her smile, the formal inclination of her head as she jotted down each order. The elusive something about her speech, was, he decided, like a faint presence of perfume in an empty room.

He found himself wishing that he wasn't wishing that she wasn't German.

He embroidered upon the possible permutations of Alsace-Lorraine. (*GG,* 99–100)

The notion of an impediment as a component of his creation and his "wishing that he wasn't wishing that she wasn't German" qualify the ideality of his portrait, and again deflation is suggested and anticipated in relation to Anna. The use of the word "embroidered" also draws attention to the fictionalizing, fantasizing process.

Throughout this fantasizing activity, there are three levels of juxtaposition, all of them in ironic contrast: the memories of Peter's son, Jeremy, as a reminder of his present anguish and lost self; straight flashback exposition that informs us of Peter's shattering and ludicrous encounters with the first three women on the CompuMate list; and the absurd overheard conversation of the two men (whom Peter depersonalizes by thinking metonymically of them as Necklace and Bracelet) about bizarre surreptitious weapons. Both the descriptions of the conversationalists and the content of their conversations subtly introduce the notion of decay and death again, as do the details of the remembered poster of *Hitler's Hellcats* and of the security guard at *Man and His World* "*stroking* the revolver butt" in contrast to Peter's cradling "his globe of cognac" (an image associated with the glass that he creates at the end of the first section). These last two details are associated with the symbolic death of Jeremy in Peter's mind.

The third section of the story is again set around a drinking-dining scene: Peter's bizarre encounter with the penultimate woman on the CompuMate list, Elspeth McCleod, whom he sees—significantly in the context of the inventing motif—initially in terms of the manufactured facade of sophisticated modern living and as a character in a play (*GG*, 106). The entire scene is sustained on a level of simultaneously pathetic and humorous irony, from the absurdity of steaming the salmon in the dishwasher through the revelations about her ex-husband's perverse behavior to the final detail of the photograph of the "famous" junior-league hockey players. That irony is also evident in the dialogue itself, which is important not only because the jagged and ironic rhythms of the conversation reveal a failure to communicate and the essential isolation of both characters, but also because that jaggedness contrasts starkly with the smooth rhythms and wit of the later conversation between Peter and Anna.[9] The whole scene is, in fact, meant to be compared implicitly to the final scene, from the level of language down to the metonymic details of dress of the two women.

One repeated image crystallizes the pathetic isolation of these two people: "Peter looked at the white shoes, one of them standing, one lying on its side. He'd always felt absurdly moved by woman's shoes. Such frail shells. Compared with men's shoes, like toys. Glass slippers. . . " (*GG*, 112). Later in the bathroom:

He thought of the fallen white shoes, one standing, one lying on its side.
Sad he; sad she.
. . . . . . . . . . . . . . . . . . . . . . . . . . . . . . . . . . . . . . . . . . . . . . . . . . . . . . . . . . . . . . . . . . .
"Poor sad Peter Thornton," he whispered to the furry floor, "what are you doing in this sad lady's house?" (*GG*, 115–16)

This image is strategically followed by an allusion to Robert Louis Stevenson's "Requiem," the last lines of which—

> Here he lies where he longed to be,
> Home is the sailor, home from sea,
> And the hunter home from the hill—

served as an epitaph on Stevenson's tomb atop Mt. Vaea in Samoa: "He would have liked to have stayed in the bathroom, read, gone to sleep on the carpet. Leaning forward was making him dizzy. He consulted his watch. Sitting on the furry seat was like what sitting on a St. Bernard would be like. Which would rescue him and take him home and give him aspirins and milk. He stared at the tiled wall. Home, he thought, for no good reason, is the sailor home from sea, and the hunter home from the hill" (*GG*, 116). The desire for sleep, for home, is, in other words, an implied desire for death born out of the weariness of life. Again, the idea of death invades the story, and perhaps there is even an association in terms of death between Stevenson and Stevens, Anna's surname.

The final section of the story is important in terms of pacing. Metcalf slowly and suspensefully builds us up only—staggeringly, excruciatingly, ironically—to bring us down. More than the three previous sections, this final part reveals Metcalf as a master of ironic effect. It begins with another restaurant scene and with Peter's ironic decision to abandon his quest and to restructure his life by embracing the single life. This so-called decision to face reality, however, is immediately undercut by his fictionalizing of, once again, a waitress:

His waitress was the large woman. He watched her making out the bill. He was pleased he'd got her and not the small, Heidi-like one. . . . The large woman's handsome face had reminded him of some other face and the likeness had troubled him for months until he'd recognized it as the impassive gaze of the woman in Giorgione's *Tempesta*. The resemblance was striking. She frowned as she figured the tax from the table on the back of her pad. He imagined her as in the painting, naked, babe at breast . . . he saw himself the painting's other character, that enigmatic youth against the violent sky. (*GG*, 121–22)

The allusion to Giorgione is significant; for he was, as G. C. Argan, an art historian, has said, a painter who conceived of a painting as a poem, "a mysterious moment filled with suspense, as if in expectation of some decisive natural event"[10]—our moment in the story awaiting the "natural event" of Anna's death—and, in terms of that event, the enigmatic figures and threatening skies of the *Tempesta* analogically introduce appropriate suggestions of the ominous.

The next movement of this section focuses emphatically on Peter's despondency and psychological "amputation"; he is no longer a whole man. Metcalf brings us down here to intensify the following movement up toward Anna. Peter's inability to see clearly the face of his wife in the imagined winter scenario (an effect not unlike the earlier analogy to the fading snapshots of his son, Jeremy) and his failure to remember, to "invent," her body not only stress his

88 JOHN METCALF

utter isolation, but also indicate that she has lost "reality"—in terms of fictional truth—for him; she is no longer part of his personal mythology:

> He tried to remember her body, tried to remember making love, but she, his wife, Pat, dissolved, faded, assumed the postures of models in *Penthouse* and *Cavalier*.
> He wondered why he felt so sad, her real face gone, her real body. The moving men remained more vivid, past drama more acute than present feelings. (*GG,* 123)

Then, because he must read "the final chapter," because he must find "a fitting conclusion to his dismal adventure," because "this was not the way that stories ended," he decides to phone the last name on the CompuMate list, Anna Stevens: "He felt about it, he decided, as he did when he stayed up late to finish a detective story. The action and the minor characters intrigued him but towards the end of the book exhaustion dragged him down and all that remained was the tedium of the explanation—a scene always contrived, the villain revealing all before pulling the trigger, the cast assembled in the library. Tedious, often silly, but essential before he could brush his teeth and go to bed" (*GG,* 125). As an ironic analogy to the end of the story, Peter's expectations here are horifyingly mocked.

The implied values of "Bach or Vivaldi" in the background and the sound of Anna's voice (which associates her with the German waitress) provide the impetus for Peter's intense creation of Anna:

> But mainly he thought about her voice. Ever since his adolescence he'd been oddly excited by women with a certain kind of voice and she had it. "Husky" did not describe it; that was the property of torchsingers and the like. "Deep" or "low" did not do it justice. For some reason he had come to associate the timbre with coolness, the coolness of moss, of ancient masonry, and over the years had imagined a scene which was somehow the equivalent of the voice.
> At a cocktail party, he was introduced to a beautiful woman. They talked. He was holding her glass while she searched her purse for matches. Before taking the glass back, she placed her forefinger across the inside of his wrist for a second. Her finger was slim and cool. The touch was almost solemn yet shockingly erotic because proprietorial. A cool finger across the heat of his pulse, a sophisticated "yes."
> And that was the sound of the voice. (*GG,* 126–27)

The forefinger across the wrist is ironically echoed at the end of the story when it descends into the reality of the nicotine-stained finger of the physician, Forbes: "Peter stared at Forbes' forefinger as it lay across the inside of Anna's wrist. The finger was bright yellow with nicotine. He tried to read the expression on the man's face. The face told him nothing" (*GG*, 151). The "image" has been stained; innocence has descended into experience; ideality has been shattered into reality.

The letter that Peter writes, in which "he wove all necessary information about himself into the fabric of his chronicle of mis-adventure," stresses his fictionalizing of his life, his creation of himself; and it is to this invention, which Peter sees as ideal truth, as truth emotionally and psychologically superior to the factual truth of reality, and which parallels the level of truth in his creation of Anna, that she responds:

He wrote and rewrote, shading an emphasis here, burnishing a highlight, lengthening there, excising. Humour with a dash of pathos dealt with Stella Bluth and Nadja Chayefski. Elspeth McCleod he played as comedy degenerating into farce. He himself emerged as a slightly bruised idealist, rueful, the Philip Marlowe of the antique trade, a man unafraid to admit to loneliness, a man, who, in these untender times, was not ashamed to admit to the possibility of love.

Love, which, strip away our sterile sophistication, our bright brittleness, was perhaps . . . etc., etc.

Difficult, this part. Such rhetoric clashed with the letter's general tone. He struggled to bring it under control. (*GG*, 129)

Significantly, his feelings of disorientation upon completing the letter are those of many fiction writers, but they also foreshadow the disorienting descent from the ideal to the real at the end of the story (*GG*, 129). The adumbration of a descent into reality is also suggested in the detail of Alan's telephone call, which interrupts Peter's fantasizing—"Really, North!" said Peter. "Must you sully everything you touch?" Immediately after this conversation follows Peter's "part dream and part memory" of his innocent failure to kiss an idealized girl of his childhood that also anticipates the ultimate deflation of Anna.

Anna's written reply to his letter, filled with promise, intensifies Peter's fantasizing of her, reaching a pitch in the exotic, romantic fantasy of Peter and Anna together in Spain and in his idyllic

"picture" of "them together, a family again, Anna and Jeremy, on
picnics, at the seaside, in fields full of flowers" (*GG,* 135). This
vision is significant not only because it indicates that Peter's quest
is a desire to regain his lost Edenic identity as husband-father, but
also because it posits Anna as a symbolic surrogate of his ex-wife
Patricia. Metcalf further associates the two women by the detail of
the red coat: the "scarlet winter coat" of Patricia's that Peter discovers in the carton that the movers had left, and Anna's remark
on the phone, "I'll be the one . . . carrying a copy of *Pravda* and
a saxophone and wearing a red coat" (*GG,* 137). In view of the
destruction of the "reality" of both Patricia and Anna, it is significant that neither is a "girl in gingham."

It is impossible to convey the power of the final movement of
the story, the quality and texture of the scene as it moves toward
the bitter irony of Anna's horrifying death, but a few important
details that contribute to the horror of the effect should be singled
out. For example, several details, once again, anticipate the ultimate, shattering descent into reality: 1) the restaurant, which Peter
has chosen as an approximation of an ideal setting, has, "to his
horror," been remodeled; 2) Peter's imagining of "the whole restaurant as a bad stage set for a musical," which is also a detail
associated with the earlier references to soap opera and low-grade
comedy; 3) the thick, nasty taste of his drink as he waits for Anna;
4) the fateful blizzard that will later prevent the ambulance from
arriving on time, the fatefulness of the anaphylactic shock occurring
because, no doubt, of an allergy to seafood, and Peter's ironic remark
that he is "one who is Captain of his Fate"; and 5) the hood of
Anna's red coat catching "on the fluke of an anchor" and the awkwardness of her maneuver around the barrel.

Many other details also contribute to the overall ironic effect: the
obvious irony of their total compatability; their discussion of the
"drama of families," which draws attention to the fictionalizing
motif—as does the discussion about fakes and frauds in the antique
business, the irony that Peter's task as an appraiser is to distinguish
between the fake and the real, and the details of Peter's dress suggesting that he is a "costumed" character. Finally, the impact of
the ending is intensified by the humiliating and horrifying reality
of Anna's death—sweat, vomit, urine, and diarrhea—by the doctor's description of anaphylactic shock as "drowning from the inside," a remark that suggests a psychological as well as a physical

death; by the emotional disparity created by the doctor's matter-of-fact demeanor; and by the painful incongruity of the routineness of the final scene with the waitress and the excruciating irony of her final remark, which signals closure:

> A voice said something.
> "Pardon?"
> A waitress stood there with an order pad.
> "Are you the party that was at this table before?"
> He nodded.
> "The other girl she's finished her shift. She's gone off now."
> He stared at her.
> She was middle-aged with frizzy, yellowed hair and glasses. She looked tired. Like the other waitresses, she was wearing baggy red pirate trousers and a blouse with puffed sleeves fastened at the breast with black thongs. Round her waist was a wide leather belt with a brass buckle. Stuck in the belt was a plastic flintlock pistol. She was wearing the sort of boots that are illustrated in children's stories, *Dick Whittington, The Brave Little Tailor, Puss-in-Boots.*
> "Anything else?" he repeated.
> "Yes," she said. "Something nice for dessert?" (*GG*, 154)

She is, of course, associated with all the other waitresses Peter has fantasized about and specifically with the fiction motif in the reference to children's stories, which echo the references to children's books made earlier (*GG*, 89). These remind us of his lost child, and the belt and pistol remind us of the earlier details about weapons, the security guard, and the poster of Hitler's Hellcats—metonymic signifiers of death. But her *red* pirate trousers also identify her with Patricia and Anna. The implication in the accumulation of these details perceived through Peter's consciousness is that, alas, he has reverted to fantasizing, inventing, fictionalizing again.

The story generates many meanings: perhaps when the ideal, when art, is incarnated in reality, it either ceases to be ideal, ceases to be art, or is destroyed; perhaps there are two realities that can never meet; perhaps innocence must always descend into experience; perhaps man is a victim of his fantasies.

## Private Parts

Focusing on the sexual and psychological drama of the childhood and adolescence of one T. D. Moore, a minor Canadian poet, *Private*

*Parts: A Memoir* is one of the most richly textured and subtle of John Metcalf's fictions. The novella is a first-person narrative in which the "I" represented in the discourse (enounced)—significantly the narrator is named only once, indirectly—is forever sliding away from the "I" doing the speaking (enunciation), as the narrator himself realizes in the metanarrative moments that punctuate the text at strategic intervals throughout the story, thus making us conscious that we are reading a story and intensifying our engagement with it as a construction but thereby opening up gaps in the discourse. He is also aware (on numerous occasions he speaks about words and their meanings, signifiers and their signifieds) that the signified is forever slipping beneath the signifier, resisting our attempt to locate and delimit it.[11] *Private Parts* is an interrogative text, to use Catherine Belsey's term:[12] a fictional discourse about language and about how the "self" is constituted in discourse and how the world becomes, as in Joyce Cary's fiction, metonymic facets of the narrator's character.

There is a rich play on the words *private, parts,* and *self* throughout this autobiographically structured story, which is itself a play on both the conventions of memoir and the bildungsroman and *Kunstlerroman,* the novel of formation and the artist novel. The narrative is a telling of the private, nonpublic part of his life, his so-called inner psychological and emotional life, his private, hidden self— those effaced aspects of self kept intact and preserved, his mythologized lost life of youth. Self is, however, metonymically equated with private parts, with the penis, early in the story, and so the narrator's "feelings of 'penile inadequacy' " (*PP,* 58) resulting from his childhood vision of "Bobby's thing," reaching "nearly to his knee" and "fat" as his arm (*PP,* 11), are feelings of insecurity and doubt that persist from the beginning to the end of the story. Thus masturbation, "self-abuse," the sin against the Holy Ghost who is for the narrator the private parts, the penis, of the Trinity, is a metonym of exploration of the self, of one's private parts. As his masturbatory acts begin to focus on outward images, as he moves away from a narcissistic phase, he begins to develop socially.

The narrative is externally structured into two parts—the first subdivided into twelve sections, some of which are further subdivided by asterisks; the second, into three sections, the first of which is subdivided by asterisks. The first part is a series of sequences of "anecdote and reflection" (*PP,* 17) that chronicle the equivocal growth of the narrator's sense of "self" in psychological, sexual, social, and displaced artistic terms—all of which are in a metonymic relationship to each other. The second part is a disturbing meditation on the meaning and effects of the first part.

One appropriate way to read the story is in terms of Jacques Lacan's paradigm of the child's entry into language and society, a passage which involves a realization of loss, absence, and difference.[13] Language is impersonal and both precedes and exceeds us as individuals. It is not something we each bring with us into the world at birth, but—as the very first section of the story makes clear in the narrator's response to his uncle's language and to the discrepancy between his uncle's private and public self—an institution into which we are gradually initiated in childhood as the most basic component in all our socialization. Language is, as Ferdinand de Saussure argued, a "social fact." Some of our libido, in Lacan's Freudian terms, must be given up to the system. We must pass from the "private," if also delusive, order of what Lacan calls the Imaginary to the social order of the Symbolic though the Imaginary continues to operate even after our inscription into the Symbolic. *Private Parts* traces this fall, this journey, and its effects of loss, absences, and difference.

In the Lacanian Imaginary state, summarized in the early narcissistic "minor stage," a phase between six and eighteen months, I look in a mirror and recognize what I see there, the image of my own body, as myself ("it's me"), as an "ideal unity," rather than as a reflection optically produced. But no matter how it may appear in the Imaginary, identity is never simply itself ("it's me") but is forever only a likeness, a reflection of something else. Consequently, identity is only possible as *misrecognition*. Yet even though the image in the mirror is not me, I must nevertheless identify myself with it because it is only there and nowhere else that I can be present to myself at all. Misrecognition is necessary since I can have no other identity, and without identity I cannot speak. As in Lacan, the mediating role of the body in this process of constituting the subject is stressed in Metcalf's synecdoche of private parts.

In the Symbolic order, a network of linguistic, discursive, and social rules, we ourselves can never be more than an "event" or grammatical act, not an essence. The ego, the "self," cannot be transcendent, for it is brought about as a position in a discourse. In terms of vision, I can only identify myself in a mirror by seeing this reflection from somewhere else. In terms of language, I can only identify myself in discourse by speaking about this character called myself from somewhere else. The "I" in discourse is always sliding away from the "I" doing the speaking, the "I" speaking from somewhere else.

The fixed position of the ego is only a temporary point in the process of what Lacan calls the Other—the rest of language, all the absences and dependencies in the Saussurean vertical or paradigmatic chain that have to be barred in discourse in order for meaning to take place along the Saussurean syntagmatic or horizontal chain. Because language is a differential system, conscious meaning "insists" in discourse; none of its elements "consists" in the signification of which it is at the moment capable. This insistent meaning is produced as an effect of the Other, all the other possible meanings, which remains outside the discourse and is, consequently, to that extent unconscious. The unconscious is thus "the discourse of the Other," as we see, for example, in the narrator's recurring anxiety dreams of journeying and in his many implicit discussions about the dissemination of meaning in words. The repressions entailed in moving from the Imaginary to the Symbolic order involve the opening up, the creation, of the unconscious and, as we see in the story, of "desire," which is infinite and insatiable; and the phallus, the figurative representation of the male organ, is for Lacan "the signifier of desire,"[14] the means by which all desire is organized:

> *It doesn't matter* that all those endearingly innocent American authorities state that an average-sized organ is preferable to one larger than average. *It doesn't matter* that women claim to prefer organs in the normal range. *It doesn't matter* that the average length of the vagina in a sexually aroused woman is only 4½ inches. *It doesn't matter* that I'm married happily, the father of four children. *I don't care* what my wife and other women say, have said.
>
> *I have seen Bobby and I know what I know. I KNOW my thing is small. I know that hidden in all the trousers around me are huge organs. In every public convenience happy extroverts stand back from the urinals cosseting with justifiable pride members which to me seem to fall into the 10–12 inch range while I fumble for it in my underpants, trying to find it, winkling it out.*
>
> I wish I had a big one. (PP, 66)[15]

Metcalf's "Notes on Writing a Story" is a discussion of his "pleasures" in writing the first section of *Private Parts*, "which is the whole story in capsule, and the first paragraph is, in capsule, the whole of the first section."[16] The notes stress the metonymic and metaphoric patterns at work, the materiality of language, the intertextuality of all texts (foregrounded here through the specific references to other written texts and paintings), the paradigmatic status of his narrator's end of innocence in his sight of the naked idiot, Bobby (the farm is situated in the Eden valley, and behind the farmhouse is an apple tree), and the way the meaning of any utterance is disseminated: the notion of meaning as a self-effacing "trace" constituted by all the absent meanings whose differences from the present signified invest that signified with its apparent identity, all the other possible meanings which are the condition of this meaning. This idea of the "trace" is most obvious in Metcalf's discussion of "lisle" and "Lyle" and "Palmer" (*N*, 69). Otherness is implicit in language, and the otherness of meaning is also evident in the narrator's reference to "haunting words like 'fustian' and 'coulter,' 'stoup' and 'flitch,'" signifiers whose historical materialism is "redolent of another age" and metonymic signifiers of Uncle Fred and Aunt Lizzie but of "whose meanings" he is not "exactly sure" (*PP*, 6). An appropriate concern for a writer, this emphasis on the precedence of the signifier throughout the story is one of its most noticeable features. "Words are things before they become words, and they become things again when they do."[17]

The first paragraph of the story is, as Metcalf indicates, a microcosm of the first section and, in turn, of the whole in that it begins with high expectations. The first sentence is a grabber: "One of my earliest sexual memories, more vivid and perhaps more important than any subsequent sexual memory, is of my Uncle Fred and the idiot" (*PP*, 6). But the promised drama ends with death and the loss of innocence: a literal death at the end of the first paragraph, loss of innocence at the end of the first section, and a metaphorical death, a lost sense of self at the end of the story. The patterns of juxtapositions and antitheses, manifestations of the general structure of deflation and diminution, are also established in the first section: innocence and knowledge, "a golden past and a hideous present, a fertile landscape and a barren landscape and . . . a rural peace and an urban violence" (*N*, 69). Finally, in the vision of "Bobby's thing" accompanied by guilt and remorse we have the initiating impulse of the narrative that shapes the narrator's sexual life, his "self": he will never be able to live up to, come to terms with, the phallic image of Bobby—it is thus a signifier of desire—despite his search through various displaced forms of redemptive art.[18]

In the second section we learn of the "pious, sour, and thin" (*PP*, 12) Wesleyan world in which he dwells as a child, the "burden of guilt and conviction of sin . . .—dirtiness, death, disapproval, impurity—" that "eventually became the front line of the ravaged battlefield" of his "adolescence" (*PP*, 17). At the end of the section, however, the narrator breaks the fictional illusion of a continuous narrative, thus reminding us that we are reading a constructed discourse, to comment metanarratively on the writing. The story thus shifts to a new narrative level, and the narrative up to this point becomes second degree.[19] Again we see the "I" of the discourse slipping away from the "I" of the speaking event as the narrator struggles with the instability of the identity between signifier and signified, especially in the word *tortured:*

> And what can you understand by my use of the word 'tortured'?
> Did you think I meant—'troubled'?
> The fault is mine. I have pictured my mother as a joyless puritan. But this is not the whole truth. The fault lies in my writing, feelings hidden behind humour, pain distanced by genteel irony. The truth is ugly and otherwise. My father was merely eccentric; my mother was mad.
> Her mind festered. It was a pit of unimaginable filth—a contagion I did not escape. I hated her. I am happy she is dead.
> Had I not been stronger, had I not battled her every day of my life, I could well have joined my brothers in institutions the world over, those who mutilated their genitals with shards of glass, or worse, the ones who came in judgement and cut off tits with butchers' knives, carved cunts with cleavers. (*PP*, 17–18)

Returning to the first narrative level, he tells us that he vowed that his "life would be filled with laughter, beautiful women, warm flesh," that it "would be lived in the sun" (*PP*, 18).

In the next section he has his "first encounter with Art" (*PP*, 18), which, as might be expected, is generally inimical to his Wesleyan world, in the performance of the monologuist, Mr. Montague (who, as his checkered suit suggests, is a displaced version of Evelyn Waugh) (*PP*, 21–22). He is especially drawn to the power of inference generated in Mr. Montague's ability to perform a variety of different "voices."

Although permeated with a humor that controls the potential for sentimentality, the next few sections mark "an intensification of the warfare" (*PP,* 22) with his mother and the emergence of "the first counter-moves of his self-shaping" (*PP,* 22), as his sexual life moves to a "focus on sexual images of the outer world" (*PP,* 25–26). Again, we see a concern with the "power of words," the precedence of signifiers, and the slipping of signifieds under signifiers:

A boy of thirteen lives possessed and I use the word in its biblical sense. Such words as 'desire' or 'lust' are pallid counters for the raw actuality. *Frenzy* or *fever,* with their medical connotations, are more appropriate. (*PP,* 27)

The word itself, 'bodice' was only just bearable; such a word as 'nipple' was beyond endurance; the black letters on the white page blurred into an aura, an aureole of shimmering desire so intense that further reading was impossible and we would stare into space bereft of our wits. (*PP,* 29)

Much of my early reading was merely the search for erotic incident. Two fragments lodge in my mind yet. One, 'he toyed with her bubbies' was presumably from some eighteenth-century novel. The other, 'she made him free of her narrow loins' was the first of many intense pleasures given me by Evelyn Waugh. (*PP,* 29)

He continues to live in "a world of constant guilt, anxiety and self-loathing," his "mother's handmaidens" (*PP,* 31), culminating in her grotesque repudiation of him after her discovery of his copy of *Health and Efficiency,* a nudist magazine, her tirade humorously but pathetically undermined by his mournfully wanking himself to sleep. His mother's white net gloves become an emblematic focus for all his hatred of her and their way of life, a symbol of everything from which he wants to escape. It is no surprise, then, to learn that when he returns to England for her funeral, he burns those net gloves together with her little silken bags of lavender, with which he also identifies her.

Around age fourteen or fifteen he encounters the "Second Coming of Mr. Montague" (*PP,* 39) in his discovery of the book *The March of the Moderns* by art historian William Gaunt through which his attraction to Art is intensified. He does not wish to seek Art for its own sake, however, but because it represents the antithesis of his Wesleyan world and is also a potential vehicle of escape and power, fame and sex (*PP, 39*). From a pseudointerest in painting, he moves through his friend Tony to an interest in jazz because it too is associated with the subversive. But the prolepsis (a narration of a story-event at a point before earlier events have been mentioned) that reports his disillusioning trip to New Orleans is in its deflating, disillusioning pattern an anticipation of the final diminution or deflation.

During this jazz phase he has his "first brush with a girl's private parts" (*PP, 53*): his bizarre sexual encounter with Helen who has been, paradoxically, sexually aroused because of her experience at a Billy Graham revival. The experience precipitates his release: "I, who was destined for great things, I, whom the Muse had claimed, had squandered two years of my valuable life on a girl with fat lips, on a girl who probably thought Ezra Pound was a kind of cake, on a girl *who had been genuinely moved by Billy Graham's trombonist*" (*PP, 57*).

Part 1 ends with an intensification of this reductive pattern in his disturbing response to some pornographic photographs, which were not "erotic" in their effect but "deadening":

I kept returning to one particular picture; it disturbed me profoundly. A mattress lay on the floor. On the extreme edge of the picture was a toe-cap, a shoe belonging perhaps to the man holding the spotlight above the scene. One woman held in her hand a long animal's horn, the tip of which she was inserting into the other woman's vagina. The animal's horn was about two and a half feet long and spiral in form, the horn perhaps of some kind of antelope. The face of the woman into whom this was being inserted was partially obscured by the domino mask but she seemed to be smiling. (*PP, 58*)

Again, he experiences another disturbing phallic image, associated with "Bobby's thing," another signifier of insatiable desire, a desire never to be fulfilled.

Part 2 is a reflection on the meaning of the chronicle related in part 1. Because he has early identified the "self" with penis, a part with whole—a double misrecognition—"Anxiety has been the constant in 'his' sexual career," an anxiety that finds unconscious expression in an inability to "distinguish between real and imagined events" (*PP*, 60), complemented so many times by his metanarrative comments about truth in language and his awareness of shifting signifieds in the words he uses: "A story told me or a story I've invented often becomes more real than an event I know to have occurred. And increasingly, I find myself doubting even those certainties" (*PP*, 60). Is the image in the mirror really me? Is the "I" in discourse really me? Whether heard, invented, or "factual," the event is produced by discourse; and subjects are events, are constituted, only in discourse.

Once again, we read of instances of deflations, types of the whole, in his daughter's description of his penis as a finger and in his wife's undermining remark, which he records after the rhetorically heightened quotation from John Cleland (". . . it stood an object of terror and delight"), "my wife says she thinks they look silly" (*PP*, 62). And again, the narrative ruptures the established narrative level to move to a new level of narration, an apparent confessional mode, only for that mirror to be also shattered:

Style betrays me.
    An easily-written kind of humor, five-finger exercise.
    My heart isn't in it.
    "Truth," as my mother always used to say, "will out."
    *It doesn't matter* that all those endearingly innocent American authorities state that an average-sized organ is preferable to one larger than average. . . . I wish I had a big one.
                                    *
How neatly the rhetoric of that confession is managed! How prettily worked its repetitions, its movements in and out of italic.
    Lies. Mainly lies.
    So much of my life is spent alone in silence creating illusions that even when I set out to tell the truth I cannot escape the professional gestures, the hands turned palms-and-backs to the audience, the cuffs pulled wide to illustrate emptiness—then the sudden string of flags.
    I am not confessing here merely to "penile inadequacy" but to the continuing power of that disapproval of and distate for 'self'—for me— to the continuing power of those ghostly commands:
    *Wash yourself.*
    *Dry yourself.*
    Why must disappointment all I endeavour end? (*PP*, 65–67)

Is the image in the mirror really me? Is the "I" in the discourse really me? Is the "I" in the recurring "dream of journey" really me? It is certainly a speaking of the Other, the language of the unconscious—dissynchronization, alienation, and fragmentation: broken chocolate bar machines, hanged friends, always late and out of place.

After his loss of virginity, despite all the "new Anxieties as the fashions changed" (*PP*, 69), sex becomes ordinary, perhaps even less than ordinary, reduced to once a week while the children watch *"Sunshine Saturday on ABC"* (*PP*, 69). Because nothing will ever again approximate the sexual melodrama of his adolescence, because his present is impoverished, he, like his friend Gerry, mythologizes the past: "We always talked about the past, things that happened twenty years and more ago, old wounds, old friends, old grievances, the two who were already dead, as though we could only be comfortable in mythology, in events upon which time had imposed some imaginable order. We seem to live there more brightly than in our present, with more enthusiasm than we would in our imaginable future" (*PP*, 71). His parents remain "giant figures in a glaring stage, their lives the myth of my life" (*PP*, 75), and when he returns to Croyden years later, he does not try to find his friend Tony or make enquiries about him: "I wanted to remember him for always and ever as the boy who imagined sucking the hair in Eliska's armpit" (*PP*, 71).

He does return to Yorkshire, however, but only to find it "shrunken, mild-mannered, ordinary" (*PP*, 78), this trip, like the dream and the entire narrative, a journey into the present deflated reality. The manse of his childhood, "that mansion with its many rooms, turned out to be a seedy Victorian house" (*PP*, 78), and the scarlet woman his mother warned him about turns "out to be a lonely old woman who drank too much gin too early in the day" (*PP*, 78). All of these depressing recognitions are complemented by the only quite ordinary "writer of sorts" he has become (*PP*, 76–77). Then we see that because he is "burned out" (remember the burning of his mother's gloves and lavender), he lives vicariously through his wife: "Mary's life fascinates me; I love to observe all her drama and silliness. I often feel she's more *alive* than I am; sometimes I even feel I live *through* her" (*PP*, 79).

He is also alienated from his children: "They're children from another world, a world in which I'm alien, the New World" (*PP*, 81). Like the Brontës who wrote among the ghosts at Haworth parsonage, he too feels that he lives his "life among ghosts" and that the stories he writes "are exorcisms" (*PP,* 82):

The dead are all around me. I am too much part of them.
*Wash yourself.*
*Dry yourself.*
It's as if I exhausted all my passion by the age of sixteen; nothing since has compared with the drama and intensity of that battle of wills, a titanic struggle fought against the backdrop of Hell.
And none of it now means anything I can understand; I no longer believe in the fire and ice of Hell and sex is what happens on Saturdays. (*PP,* 82–83)

Eden can never be recovered. There is only boredom and disillusionment.

The story ends openly with his taking out of his sextant which he has smuggled into the house and kept hidden: "As the washing-machine changed rhythm and the water drained away I took the sextant out. It sits in a mahogany box, the brass and glass nestled in green baize. I looked at it, at its telescope, index mirror, and horizon glass. I turned the clamp screw and the tangent screw enjoying the feel of the milled edges. I'm not quite sure how it's supposed to work" (*PP,* 84).

The meaning of the sextant is "overdetermined," dispersed among innumerable possibilities. It is an iconic image that serves as a condensation: a sole idea represents several associative chains at whose point of intersection it is located. It is, of course, a phallic symbol, a signifier of desire, and that it is smuggled into the house and kept hidden suggests that it is a "private part," a symbolic substitute for his penis, something for him to play with, an unconscious link to his past. It is also an image of "self," then, another misrecognition. Notice, too, the trace of *sex* in the word and that it is an instrument of *journeying,* used to seek direction on the sea, that measures the angular distance between two objects, the sun and the horizon, by a double reflection from two *mirrors*[20]—details which remind us of the illusions of "self" presented throughout the narrative and the Lacanian paradigm. The final sentence reiterates the dominant motifs of uncertainty and doubt: "I'm not quite sure how it's supposed to work" (*PP,* 84).

# Chapter Six
# Novels

For Metcalf, the novel is a loose, accommodating form in contrast to the intensity and compressed effects of both the short story and the novella. It is thus a particularly apposite medium for presenting comic set pieces of a satiric nature exhibiting the skills of caricature and the grotesque. In a strict sense, however, neither *Going Down Slow* nor *General Ludd,* Metcalf's two novels, is satire, for neither is satirically didactic in the sense of generating an inspiration to re-model social structures and establishing, implicitly or explicitly, concrete alternatives or norms. Whatever norms there are in these texts are themselves decayed or corroded, residing in the past. They exist only as absences in the other. Rather, it would be more accurate to describe both novels as forms of invective—which, like satire, also use humor, ridicule, and hyperbole but for different ends— grounded morally in an anarchist ideology. Both novels suggest, for example, that Metcalf would agree with the anarchist argument represented by Max Stirner that the most appropriate response to the authoritarian system (here the Canadian educational system and North American capitalism) is rebellion, which is an individual act, rejecting the repressiveness of the system and expressing one's free-dom. The object of rebellion for Stirner is the system's collapse, whereas in contrast the object of revolution, which involves sub-merging one's individuality, is to replace the system by a different one. Such a revolutionary aim would be the satirist's but not that of the writer of comic invective whose real aim would be the rebel's— that is, the destruction of the system. Metcalf's anarchism, however, like George Woodcock's, is not a praxis, but a critical perspective.[1]

In a letter written to Doug Rollins in May 1966, six years before the publication of *Going Down Slow,* Metcalf speaks of seeing in such anarchists as Proudhon and Stirner a confirmation of a position toward which he had been moving: ". . . the complete anarchist would say that you must never compromise your original position to achieve a partial success. *Instead* you are totally justified as an *individual* to keep on repeating your original position. This magnificent refusal to be influenced by the practicalities surrounding a moral position seems important to me. The virtue lies in the kind of personal honour—group honour or 'rightness' being only the sum of individual rightnesses. Compromise seems more and more to be the beginning of corruption. In a way, this is really what my novel is about."[2] The novel to which he refers here is the short novel, *The Lady Who Sold Furniture*, and in some ways *Going Down Slow* and *General Ludd* are in fact rewritings of that novella since all involve the problematic of integrity and compromise vis-à-vis personal relationships and the educational system.

## *Going Down Slow*

The surface structure of *Going Down Slow* is a comically devastating assault on the puerility of secondary school education, but in the young teacher's ultimate capitulation to an absurd system—both North American vulgar capitalism and the Greater Montreal Protestant School Board—is the deep structure of a story about integrity, corruption, and compromise, about the psychological death resulting in capitulation to social structures or institutions that are inherently destructive of individuality. For David Appleby, like his two best friends, but unlike his student lover, Susan, finally does succumb, does implicitly sell out for a career and financial security and, as a result, is symbolically poisoned. Despite the brilliant comic set pieces, however—the real strength of the novel—the central narrative line is not really strong enough to sustain our abiding interest as a form of classical realism, and it is, moreover, rather conventional: one more example in a long list of young men who compromise.[3] A number of scenes, for instance, have only a metonymic, not a direct narrative, relationship to the central story line, yet they are inherently interesting in themselves. Many of them, in fact, in their relative autonomy could be read as short stories. Indeed, chapter 5 appeared with very minor changes as the story "Flowers that Bloom in the Spring" in *The Teeth of My Father*.[4]

David Appleby, a young British immigrant teaching at Merrymount High in Montreal, is, like Jeanne in *Lady*, another of Metcalf's Caryesque medium-less artists whose creative urges take the form of having a love affair with a student and if not subverting then circumventing the educational system whenever feasible. The point of view is a third-person center of consciousness through which we experience his caricaturing of Susan's parents, his landlord, and most of his colleagues. These portraits are in themselves amusing, but they also serve as metonyms of David's character, indexing his attitudes and values through his varying levels of ridicule and characterizing the absurdity of the world in which he finds himself both inside and outside school.

Early in the novel Metcalf spends a considerable amount of space establishing, through both direct report (*GDS*, 20–21) and virtual report (*GDS*, 17), the "unfunny vaudeville" of, the filth and vileness of the world of, "Monsieur idle sodding Gagnon" (*GDS*, 17), his landlord. He does so because it is into this world that David finally, ironically, allows himself to be led at the end of the novel. Metcalf also spends considerable space detailing the petty, regimented, and repressive world of the high school and caricaturing such teachers as Hubnichuk, "The Boor No. 666 of Merrymount High" (*GDS*, 43); Follett, "The obscene little rotundity" (*GDS*, 41); and Brunhoff, who is "gripped by carnal thingies" (*GDS*, 60). But the two who receive the most attention are Vice-Principal McPhee and Howie Bunceford. McPhee, the "Gestapo dwarf" (*GDS*, 25), because he is the main agent of repression, moves out of the realm of caricature beyond humor to the realm of the grotesque, the disgusting, the fearsome. Ludicrous smallness and gross evil are one in McPhee. But Howie Bunceford, the head of the English Department, who "always reminded David of the expression 'a sack of shit' " (*GDS*, 88), is not just an implementer of "the Board's Condition Evaluation System, counting the sets of *Moonfleet* and *Cue for Treason*, poring over *Ancient Myths Retold for Modern Youth*, deliberating over grubby copies of *On the Edge of the Something Forest or Jungle* by creepy Albert Schweitzer" (*GDS*, 87); Howie is also, alas, "a poet" (*GDS*, 88–89).

Three main issues within the school world crystallize the problematic of integrity and compromise and prefigure the final issue of McPhee's discovery of the affair between David and Susan. The absurdity of the bowdlerized edition of Hugh MacLennan's *Two Solitudes*—"with Introduction, Notes and Questions by Claude T. Bissell M.A. Ph.D."—is epitomized by Question four:

*Marius is a study in abnormality. In Section 5, does MacLennan adequately account for his attitudes and action?*

A judicious question. A question, David decided, which for sheer nerve, was worthy of some form of award.

As Marius was motivated by guilty lust for his stepmother and hatred of his father for screwing said stepmother the night his first wife died, and, as both facts had been bowdlerized entirely in Section 5, the question indicated an advanced lack of shame on the part of Claude T. Bissell M.A. Ph.D.

Or possibly a black sense of humour? (*GDS,* 125)

The ludicrousness of the situation is emphasized in David's time-consuming restoration of the original text through mimeographed sheets only to have the following questions put to him:

"Mr. Appleby?"

"Yes, Carl?"

"If we use this information on the exam, will we be penalized?"

"What do you mean? Why should you be?"

"Well, we're not supposed to be reading it and maybe the Examiner'll take marks off."

"And Mr. Appleby?"

"Yes, Mary?"

"What if the Examiner hasn't read the book—the proper one, I mean?"

"Put a note on your answers that you're referring to the complete text."

"But if we want," said Carl, "we can just refer to the school edition?"

David looked down at the wad of purple, mimeographed sheets.

"Yes, Carl," he said, "you can do that if you want." (*GDS,* 127)

The second issue involves the inappropriateness of a composition assignment David has given his students on *"The Medical Examination or The Dentist"* (*GDS,* 97) and McPhee's removal (as he subsequently learns) of certain "unsuitable" photographs of *The Family of Man,* which David has mounted in his classroom "to spark memories or feelings which he could fashion in his composition lessons" (*GDS,* 94).

The third issue, the bowdlerizing of the play, *Nighthaul,* is more important than the other two because it involves David's friend, Garry, who ("Apart from Miss Leet, who favoured Ayn Rand") "was the only teacher in the school who read books" (*GDS,* 39). Garry, the coproducer of the play, is willing to compromise and David, at least initially, is not:

"In this particular context, I think you're wrong, David. You've got to . . ."

"I haven't *got* to do *anything*. If you want to sell the play out, you go ahead."

"But you're prepared to 'sell' the kids out?" David got up and dropped the crumpled napkin onto his plate.

"If you like," he said. "I think I'm doing them a favour." (*GDS*, 48)

Garry himself, of course, sells out by acquiring an M.Ed. at McGill, without David's knowledge, and by seeking a career in guidance, even as Jim, David's roommate, sells out by going to the Ontario Institute for Studies in Education and buying a vulgar North American car. Garry also stands in antithesis to Susan (*GDS*, 118).

But David himself also succumbs—the play goes on—as he does over the composition topics by allowing Howie Bunceford to give a demonstration lesson reading and relishing in some dreadfully purple prose by Sir Compton McKenzie. The winding down of the scene suggests David's weariness, his defeat, his surrender, especially evident in his fulfilling, presumably for the first time, the janitor's request to put the chairs on top of the desks in regimental fashion and to lock the windows properly:

Turning back to the room, starting with the back row, he began putting the chairs up on the desktops. From desk to desk, placing the chairs quietly, squaring them, row after row, he worked towards the front.

Then he went back to the windows and pulled them down by the brass handles completely shut, locked them with the brass catches.

Going to the front of the room again, he started to erase the boards, working in short sweeps. When he had finished, he placed the eraser on the ledge. The yellow chalkdust on his fingertips revealed the whorls and patterns of his prints. He stood by his desk rubbing at the chalkdust with his thumb. (*GDS*, 103)

The final detail metonymically suggests his fingerprinting and imprisonment within the system. The winding down of this scene is anticipated in the winding down implicit in the washroom scene that ends the debate between David and Garry about the play already referred to (*GDS*, 49–50).

We have looked at instances of compromise and corruption only within the educational system, but they abound for David in the social structures of North America in general, metonymically significant in his abhorrence of the neon "Canadian Tire" sign outside his apartment, "a focus for all his feelings of dispossession, prejudice and xenophobia" (*GDS*, 19). The most dramatic example of fraudulence occurs in David's awareness that the so-called blues singer, Blind Foxy John, at the ersatz subcultural coffeehouse, the Delta, has plagiarized his song from a 1947 Lomax recording by Jelly Roll Morton (*GDS*, 71). Significantly, at the moment David is being ejected from the Delta, the "mangy moth-eaten" squirrel (*GDS*, 62) in the glass case he has purchased at Liebermann's shatters. He later leaves the squirrel in an A & W as a symbolic protest: "The picture grew elegiac in his mind. The plastic orange bobbing on the surface of the tank of orange liquid. The plastic-topped mushroom stools. Fluorescent acres of white plastic table-tops. The sticky, squidgy containers of ketchup and mustard. And on the clean and gleaming counter, the squirrel sitting like a reproach" (*GDS*, 75).

The squirrel represents the decrepit state in which the "natural" finds itself in this neon context and is associated with the nighthawks David notices from his apartment window but especially with the rooks that he sees in a tree in a corner of the school field and with which—in their wariness, wildness, and independence—he identifies:

> Strange how big they looked even at a distance. He liked their wariness, their wildness. If they nested near houses, unlike swallows or pigeons, they remained independent. They graced inhabited areas with their presence, their gleaming blackness, but remained aloof, suspicious.
> Tough, lordly birds. He liked their cawing; it was at once wild and homely, a sound which always brought a rush of feelings. As a child, he'd always associated them with the Northmen. Thistles, too. It seemed that rooks had always been there in his childhood round farms and houses, their *caw-caw* blending into his dreams as the light of summer evenings filtered through the curtains. (*GDS*, 155–56)

The birds thus become a prelapsarian pastoral symbol of lost innocence, childhood, England, the old world, "home," and all that that implies.

The squirrel, the nighthawks, the rooks all serve as signifiers of the novel's ideological norms, but—remnants of another, lost world—they are ineffective in this world of women with curlers and green garbage bags (*GDS*, 157). Their power, like David's, is diminished—exemplified not only in his compromises but subtly in his irritation about not knowing what kind of tree the rooks frequent in the school field (*GDS*, 153). They are from the past, as is John Gardner—old, decrepit, eccentric—brought out of retirement to teach one class a day, the only character besides Susan who functions as a possible norm (*GDS*, 150). Susan's moral position is the only one of unequivocal integrity, a total lack of compromise:

". . . a minute ago you said 'They can't touch me.' What did you mean by that?"

"I meant that I know who I am. I don't want to go to university or have a 'career' because it makes you into a different kind of person." . . .

"But you can't expect *not* to change, can you?"

No, of course not. But I'm going to become more me. I'm not going to have me changed to fit in with them."

"Well . . . I don't know . . . I mean, are people *really* that much changed by going to university or doing an interesting job? Distorted by it?" (*GDS*, 77–78)

The answer, of course, is yes, and her final remark to David in this scene, "You shouldn't lie to yourself" (*GDS*, 80), is telling. Susan's position is no answer for David, however, for he is already within the system.

And so this scene between Susan and David signifies the beginning of the end. David finally passes the Permanent Certificate Examination, and, confronted by McPhee's knowledge of his affair with Susan, he gives in and is implicitly repudiated for his failure by Susan (*GDS*, 162). This surrender is reinforced by his admiration for Jim's "Galaxy 500," his lying to Gagnon about being part owner of the car, and his condescending to drink and eat with Gagnon "who was accountable for unforgivable past abuse and hostility" (*GDS*, 165). Jim's remarks about why he has purchased the car reveal the extent of North American corruption, and it is on the premise of this remark that Gagnon befriends David:

"What one needs," he said, "is *style*. That's the thing. None of this threadbare graduate-student stuff. Know why?"

Gagnon was slumped on a wooden kitchen chair in a patch of shade near the front door of the building.

"Because over here, you get largely what you assume you're going to get. And people give you what they assume you're worth. And on what, pray, do they base their assumptions?"

He patted the wheel. (*GDS*, 163)

The putrid, vile characteristics of Gagnon's apartment emphasize the depth of David's descent:

The smell was rank and nearly made him gag. He tried shallow breathing. Shit certainly, piss, cooking, old sweat—but the sum was greater than the parts. Gagnon went into the kitchen alcove to get glasses and David put the case of beer on a kitchen table which stood in the middle of the living room. The table-top was encrusted. Four chrome and plastic chairs. An open package of *Wonder* bread, a melted paper of butter, a bottle of *FBI Cream Soda,* a gallon tin of strawberry jam.
A pair of rubber pants hung from the TV aerial.
A once-pink armchair.
A gutted settee which sprouted yellowing tufts of kapok.
The liquor cabinet was large and baroque: glass doors with diamond-leaded panes and gold hinges, curved legs writhing with gilded scrollwork, cupid door-knobs.
He took the glass of pernod and sat down in the armchair wondering what had trapped him into being there and suffering this Gagnon who was accountable for unforgivable past abuse and hostility. Guilt that Gagnon was French Canadian? Class guilt? Defencelessness in the face of hectoring manners? As the glass touched his lips, he tried not to imagine the kitchen, tried not to think of the unspeakable French-Canadian diseases which were obviously endemic in such an apartment. Such as hookworm, ringworm, venereal disorders, tapeworm, cankers, botulism. (*GDS,* 165–66)

The novel ends with David's vomiting—symbolically poisoned from his evening of vile drink and food with Gagnon, an evening metonymically epitomizing in a causal relationship all his other compromises, and so the poisoning is also his punishment.

## *General Ludd*

*General Ludd* is even more loosely structured than *Going Down Slow,* clearly disclosing a marked preference for scene over story, dramatic tableau over narrative development. The thin narrative thread weaves together one man's quixotic war—Jim Wells, Pierrot-like poet-in-residence isolated, á là Jules Laforque, among the Philistines in a Montreal university[5]—against the new technology of communications, the electronic revolution, "A World wired," and all that implies, and a devastating satiric assault on the mores of postsecondary education and the absence of genuine culture in Can-

ada, "save in the anthropological sense" (*GL,* 131), "a country which
has been aptly described as a spiritual K-Mart" (*GL,* 158). But
again, even more intensely than in *Slow,* Metcalf, like Waugh,
indulges in satire for its own sake, imbuing it once more with an
essentially anarchist perspective, most obviously in the Luddite motif. There are no concrete alternatives in this world of frozen french
fries, plastic cups, shopping malls, videos, and communication com-
plexes ruled by mad priests in checked sports jackets; and whatever
potential norms might seem to exist—Greece, England, nineteenth-
century Canada, John Caverly, Henry Benson, Hollis, Kathy—are
seen to be defective, decayed, invented, or mythological. The only
fit stance is one of "sullen rage" (*GL,* 132), an attempt to shine
"in a naughty world" (*GL,* 257–58), which can only lead, however,
to the bin as Wells, à la Ken Kesey, discovers by the end of the
novel. But we all know who's really mad: "Don Quixote was not
only a nobler character than Sancho Panza, but, in ways that matter,
saner" (*GL,* 167).

*Ludd* is a clear example of what Susan Rubin Suleiman calls
"ideological novels": "novels that seek, through the vehicle of fiction, to persuade their readers of the 'correctness' of a particular
way of interpreting the world."[6] That, however is the book's basic
problem, despite the comic brilliance of the set scenes and the
wonderful range of caricatures and grotesques, as Metcalf himself
now seems to realize: "It's a troubled book. I was setting out to
write comedy, dark comedy admittedly, but somehow got over-
mastered by rage so that there's a blurring between Jim Wells as
character and me as writer. And this pulls the book out of sharp
focus."[7] The tone of the novel drifts from mere anger to arrogance
at times. It is a militantly antidemocratic, willfully elitist point of
view, and it ultimately lacks persuasiveness because it is—W. H.
New to the contrary—a "put-down," not a "send-up."[8]

The use of a first-person focalizer does not help matters because
the sordid vulgarity and madness of the modern technological world
become equivocal, questionable; can, in fact, be responded to as
merely the view of a biased eccentric. It lacks the persuasive power
a third-person focus and voice might have provided in the implied
distance given such subject matter. Actually, Metcalf began the
novel in the third person and then switched to the first person
because "It was a bit staid, a bit soggy. But in the first person, I

seemed somehow to be tapping into wild energy. It was a trade-off. Zip for balance."[9]

At times, the novel seems "to have pinched neck muscles," as might be said of Kingsley Amis's novels "when they settle into mere crankiness."[10] But the novel is even more like Waugh's displays of comic irritation, for Metcalf, like Waugh, one might say, does not delight in the modern world. Waugh's myth of decline also permeates *Ludd,* the idea that civilization is in a constant and accelerating state of decay, but Metcalf makes a Yeatsian modification to the myth: "I've been thinking about something *he* [Henry Benson] said . . . We were talking about culture and change . . . and Henry said, 'Perhaps we've been at the end of something for longer than we'd care to admit'. . . . Well, we're not merely at the end of something . . . Worse. Far worse than that, we're at the beginning of something else" (*GL,* 264).[11] The rough beast slouching toward Bethlehem is of course a totally wired world (*GL,* 265–66).

The myth in Waugh "accounts for the inclusive and impartial irony of his comic imagination."[12] In Metcalf, it accounts for his all-encompassing invective informed by anarchism. As David Lodge says of Waugh: ". . . when culture is seen as a process of continual decline, no secular institution or value is invulnerable: the modern is ridiculed by contrasting it with the traditional, but attempts to maintain or restore the traditional in the face of change are also seen as ridiculous, and in any case the traditional itself also turns out to be, on close scrutiny, in some way false or compromised, already infected by decay."[13]

This is exactly the case in *Ludd,* especially evident in Wells's retreat with Kathy to his house in rural Ontario during the Christmas vacation. This is no pastoral landscape, but a cold, wintry blast of reality. Hollis, Wells's neighbor, who at first might appear to represent a norm, is contaminated by the invasion of the wired world he allows in—a radio in his milk house tuned to his favorite country and western station in Watertown, New York, and a television set, an anesthetizing substitute for reality, in his living room perpetually on, turned down, not off, only "In deference to visitors" (*GL,* 181). His wife, Eva, is a member of "The Pentecostal and Charismatic Good News Mission" (*GL,* 182), and items associated with Hollis are decaying: "I looked at the neck-yoke and whippletrees before hanging them up. The wood was grey with age and weather, deeply split, the rings rust-eaten. The harness, too, was cracked, the stitching frayed where the tugs joined the split-tug. It had all belonged to Hollis' father. It might see out the lives of Paddy and Prince. But Hollis had no son to care, to mend, to start again" (*GL,* 184). Wells also dreams of restoring his house, but "the dreams remained dreams and year by year the house grew more dissolute, the domain of vermin and dry rot" (*GL,* 186). The house was outmoded, out of place, even in its own time of 1840 having been built according to Georgian design-books and thus "reproducing late into the Victorian years an architecture designed for a more gentle time and place" (*GL,* 186): "This house and its neglect—the lack of precise knowledge—these were the essence of our historical poverty. No one really knew. Few cared. Old men said, old men remembered vaguely" (*GL,* 186). But the epitomizing image of the wasteland of the modern world is Wells's memory of the dump near his house, a vision of "the end of things" (*GL,* 249–50).

Like Hollis, other characters who function as potential norms are also vitiated in some way. Henry Benson withdraws, tuning out the world by turning off his hearing aid; John Caverly, Wells's standard for poetry, is a romantic stereotype of the neglected artist who has committed suicide; and Kathy, Wells's love interest, who is supposed to represent the "balancing force of reason"—serene, reserved, modest, scholarly—is nothing more than a "walking concept" (that is, a type of character, common in didactic fiction, whose function is to represent an ethical or philosophical notion) whose values, in terms of the prevailing ideology of the novel, are tainted by her indifference to plastic and her reading of *Destructor* novels despite her awareness that they are rubbish. Metcalf knows that she is not "realized well" and that she is not "*alive* in the way that Julia Hetherington [a marvellous caricature in the novel]'s alive."[14] Wells tells us that he is in love with her, but we certainly do not see it, and we don't know why.

The myth of decline might also account in part for the attitude toward language in *Ludd* that seems to contradict the sense of the materiality of language and the precedence of the signifier so evident in Metcalf's other fiction. Here, Wells privileges a pre-Saussurean critical ideology of expressive realism, common sense, and clarity: the illusion that language is transparent, "merely the medium in which autonomous individuals transmit messages to each other about an independently constituted world of things."[15] Invoking a passage in Wordsworth's "Preface" about the blunting of "the discriminating powers of the mind" and "the degrading thirst after outrageous stimulation," Wells intones that we've lost "Dignity, clarity, cadences . . . we're left with exactly what he described—in spades" (*GL*, 70–71). Of John Caverly, he says: "The years of critical neglect were easy to explain. He was guilty of wilful clarity. His work was so lucid, so stark, that there were no thickets of grammatical ineptitude, no coverts of arcane or personal reference, no tangles of ambiguity for the critics to thresh about in and flush meaning out. Nothing could forgive the grubby shifts to which he'd been driven to keep alive. Nothing could forgive the waste of his best years" (*GL*, 134). He attacks in Orwellian fashion the Remedial Team mercilessly for their jargon not because they deserve it so much but because common sense must dismiss as unnecessary jargon any discourse that conflicts with its own. It argues instead for the "Tyranny of lucidity": "the impression that what is being said must be true because it is obvious, clear and familiar."[16] To Hardy of the Remedial Team, Wells declaims:

"So far as I am able to understand you, I said, "which is not very far, you wish me to read a poem to the students you teach and then let them ask questions. *Is* that what you mean?"
She nodded.
"Then, my good woman, you should say so."
I held her eyes with mine.
"The answer is 'No'. And may I recommend to you the use of the words *poor, foreign, ignorant, conversation,* and *working-class.* And may I recommend further, that you earnestly apply yourself to the works of H. W. Fowler, Eric Partridge, and E. B. White."
Her face had turned a mottled pasty colour, interestingly like a steamed plum pudding.
"I've *never* been so insulted!" she said.
"Then, madam, you have been extraordinarily lucky for far too long."
Her indignant buttocks marched away.
"Good God!" said Kathy. "Do you do that very often?"
"Only under the influence of drink and extreme provocation." (*GL*, 38–39)

It is thus no surprise to find Wells including McLuhan and Teilhard de Chardin in his list of "boring old farts I'd never been able to read" (*GL*, 110), though it is a bit disappointing to find

two of the modern world's greatest thinkers, Freud and Marx, just
as summarily dismissed. What an incredible failure of rhetorical
ethos. But then common sense cannot tolerate any discourse that
conflicts with its own. It is even less of a surprise to learn that
Wells believes in the myth of the Romantic poet whose creative
imagination works in mysterious ways, the idea that poems reflect
the "reality" of experience as perceived by one particularly gifted
individual who "expresses" it as a poem that enables other lesser
beings to recognize it as "true"[17] (*GL,* 66). Because "language
matters more than most things" (*GL,* 191) to Wells—at any rate,
his idea of language as expressive realism reinforced by the illusion
of transparency—it becomes the justification not only for his attack
on the Remedials but also for his repudiation of such so-called
offenders of language as Cosimo O'Gorman, the head of the Communications Arts Complex at St. Xavier University, and especially
Itzic Zemermann, one of Wells's ersatz students.

Cosimo O'Gorman, a "false priest in commercial clothing" (*GL,*
80), is a caricature who ceases to be merely funny, moving into the
realm of the grotesque, the fearsome, the monstrous, the mad. But
in pushing him along this axis, Metcalf runs the risk of obscuring
his didactic point because of the overwhelming effects of the grotesque, most evident in Cosimo's speech from the throne of the
Dome at the end of Wells's tour of CAC. The passage should be
read in its entirety (*GL,* 129–30).

The attack on Itzic Zemermann is both more vicious and more
complex in its rationale because he is, to Wells, more dangerous in
passing himself off as a poet. To begin with, Metcalf gives Itzic
hyperbolic character traits that serve as either mitigating forces
evoking shame, sympathy, embarrassment, and rampant guilt or as
"preposterous special pleading" (*GL,* 204). The impetus for Wells's
slide from the first alternative to the second comes significantly from
someone other than Wells himself, a ploy that generates the appearance of credibility and objective justification for Wells's verbal
assault, though that someone is Julia Hetherington whose own
rhetorical ethos is questionable since she is herself satirically ridiculed: "*Were* he not a Jew, *were* he not a cripple, *were* he not allegedly
subject to heart attacks, and *were* he not a survivor of concentration
camps, one would tell him to piss off" (*GL,* 204). Because Itzic
trades on his afflictions, however, and, worse, uses "poetry as a
vehicle of that trade" (*GL,* 238), violating the great tradition, Wells

finally confronts him with the truth of his awfulness, a confrontation that results in Itzic's death by a heart attack.

Wells rationalizes his reprimand by later invoking Faulkner's remarks to the effect that "the writer's only responsibility was to his art . . . that if a writer had to rob his mother he should not hesitate for the "Ode on a Grecian Urn" was worth any number of old ladies" (*GL*, 241–42). During his speech to Itzic he also invokes a couple of verses from Auden's "In memory of W. B. Yeats":

> *Time that is intolerant*
> *Of the brave and innocent*
> *And indifferent in a week*
> *To a beautiful physique*
>
> *Worships language and forgives*
> *Everyone by whom it lives;*
> *Pardons cowardice, conceit,*
> *Lays its honours at their feet.*
> (*GL*, 237)

Are these merely rationalizations, excuses for inhumane, immoral behavior? (Are Wells's thefts and rip-offs anything more than rationalizations that the system deserves it?) Perhaps. There is certainly some doubt in his own mind in his speculations about why Auden eliminated the said verses from a later version of the poem, Metcalf's strategy to lessen the callousness of his act:

"Because they were a bit doggerel, do you think? Or because the syntax is a bit scrambled? Or because of the awkwardness of that near-rhyme in the third stanza? *Or*," I said, following her into the living room, "or do you think it was that by 1965 he no longer believed in what he'd written?" . . .
  "Where are we if they're *not* true?" . . .
  "If we're *not* pardoned?" (*GL*, 263)

The novel is rich in humorous, semifarcical scenes set both inside the university and outside it at various clubs and restaurants. Both worlds are absurd whoredoms, metonyms of each other, though "the Floating World" of alcohol associated with the clubs is more tolerable for Wells. Of these, the evening at the Hetheringtons is particularly memorable, as is the evening with the Russian writers during which Wells tells them a black "fairy tale" about "the nature and workings of literary life in Canada." Fred Lindseer's bizarre tale of the Remedials is just as dark in its comedy. The novel is also rich in brilliant caricatures besides those already mentioned: Dr. Bhadwaj, Dick Hetherington and kids, Mary Merton, the Colonel, the pawnbroker, the taxi driver with a mind like a computer, Fred Lindseer, and the Russian writers, to name most of them. All the caricatures and grotesques are humorous in themselves, but they also serve as metonymic indicators of Wells's character—his value system and the way he reads the world darkly.

The logic of the novel demands that it end darkly too, an end prefigured in the recurring wardrobe/coffin/darkness details, as Wells finds himself a psychiatric patient of Dr. Chawn's at the Montreal Jewish General Hospital. He is there because Kathy has thwarted his attempt to destroy the CAC dome by hitting him on the head with her piece of quartz, a substance associated metonymically with modern technology, and, implicitly abandoned and repudiated, he is being treated for psychiatric problems presumably at her instigation. It is no less loony than the other worlds he's been in: digital watches, diagnostic tests, and "official" beginnings of seasons. Despite the "troubled" nature of the novel, it is a far more substantial piece of writing than *Slow* and reveals forcefully Metcalf's talent for comedy. He needs to go beyond didacticism, however, as Waugh does at his best, to indulge in "a joyfully insolent defiance of all reason and right"[18] in order to have a completely successful comic novel.

# Chapter Seven
# Recent Writing
## Polemical Writing

*Kicking Against the Pricks* is an important book not only because it provides some key statements about Metcalf's poetic, as we have already seen, but because it lays painfully bare the embarrassing cultural and educational deficiencies of Canada in the early 1980s. To place Metcalf's scathing diatribes accurately, however, we should view the situation in Canada that he describes as a synecdoche of cultural problems in the Western capitalist world in general. Witty, acidic, above all provocative, the nine pieces gathered here—eight essays preceded by an interview with Metcalf conducted by Geoff Hancock—are designed less to persuade than to disturb, to unsettle the Canadian literary community—to provoke a reaction of some sort. That the book has to date not elicited a major public response, outraged or otherwise, from anyone—not even those explicitly pilloried (but not in an ad hominen fashion) and alluded to in the paronomastic title of the book—sadly echoes the knell that rings throughout the book: the real problem with Canadian writing is a sociological one, a failure to produce a substantial audience for it, though substantial is obviously a relative concept. One way to state the problem would be to say that there are proportionately fewer people reading Canadian fiction than Americans reading American fiction and English reading English fiction. Another way to come at the problem is to say that Canada simply lacks an "informed, critical, and passionate" public to produce substantial art:

Good writing will come from a culture in which native readers, teachers, and students read native writers simply because it is the *normal thing* to read one's own literature.

It is at present rather difficult to read a Canadian book without feeling faintly virtuous. Our present "culture" is a subsidized and legislated culture; it must become, however narrowly, a possession of real people. (*KAP,* 61)

We are left with the ultimate question: how?

The essays are written in the tradition of the informal or familiar essay and the plain style: relaxed, subjective, at times ironic, at others bitterly humorous, with an abundant use of anecdote and illustration and a rhetorically effective aphoristic quality. All the pieces concern, in one way or another, the functional difficulties of the writer in Canada over the past fifteen years or so as they reflect on our cultural conditions in general, and they are rooted in the following neo-Leavisite premise: "It is my quaint contention that writing is a moral act. I believe that literature is one of the most important expressions of our imaginative, moral, and national life" (*KAP*, 197).

The book raises questions that everyone involved in Canadian literature should be concerned about. Yet there has been no major public response to its provocations. Why? Perhaps Metcalf's rhetorical ethos lacks authority—he is not Margaret Atwood or Robertson Davies—but the more probable reason is that, as Christopher Lasch has taught us, social criticism in our narcissistic age "has been cheapened, like everything else, by inflation. Since interest group politics invites competitive claims to the privileged status of victimization, the rhetoric of moral outrage becomes routine, loses it critical edge. . . ."[1] In other words, a rhetoric of moral outrage in the early eighties is not a wise choice. Your only audience will already be members of your interest group. Metcalf did not give up, however. Many of these same themes run through his introductions to the *Impressions* series and "The Curate's Egg," a paper that was delivered by invitation to a group of German scholars, *Gesellschaft Fur Kanada-Studien*, in March 1984; and in November 1983 he published a feature article in the *Globe and Mail*, "What Happened to CanLit?," in which many of his points in *Kicking* are reworked.

## Recent Fiction

"Single Gents Only," first published in 1982, epitomizes wonderfully Metcalf's poetic, as his own commentary on the story that accompanies its first publication suggests.[2] There is, first of all, no plot to speak of: through a third-person center of consciousness, we read of David Hendricks's being wished adieu by his parents at a train station in northern England as he is about to embark on his first journey to university. He arrives at his destination, but because he has not responded in time to the University Accommodations Officer, he must seek "alternate accommodation." He travels to Jubilee Street, meets his landlady, her present boarders, and later his new roommate, Jeremy, from Oxford. The story is concise, compressed in its effects, "poetic."

Although Metcalf does not state it in these terms, the theme of his remarks on the story concerns the metonymic principles of contiguity and cause-and-effect—the ways in which physical character traits (especially those such as clothing over which a character has control), speech (both content and style), and setting are equivalent to character; for metonymy is every bit as much as metaphor a figure of equivalence. David's mother is a clear example of Metcalfian caricature, which is of course a form of metonymy too. She is "swiftly drawn" by being metonymically "reduced to the hat that she is wearing, a hat which strikes David as both comic and embarrassing":[3] "His mother was wearing a hat that looked like a pink felt Christmas Pudding . . . secured by a hat pin which ended in a huge turquoise knob."[4] Through two levels of indirect speech, mitigated summary, and indirect discourse mimetic to some degree, her "familiar monologues are reduced to "the knit-one-pearl-one of his mother's precepts," a "reworking of the Polonius and Mr. Micawber material" (*G*, 159). But because "literary caricatures are not heavy black strokes on blank paper but heavy lines against a background that *suggests* the complexity and detail of a life . . . David's mother is further suggested by the inexpensive and rather old-fashioned scents or colognes she wears [another metonymic relationship] and by her reported monologue and almost pointless desire to know whether David secured a seat on the train" (*BC*, 175–76). Finally, later on the train, in his attempt to define differentially what he might become "by defining what he was leaving behind" (*G*, 162), his mother is involuntarily and metonymically evoked by the "hideous images" that come to his mind: "sachets of dried lavender, Post Office Savings Books, hyacinth bulbs in bowls, the *Radio Times* in a padded leather cover embossed with the words *Radio Times,* Sunday best silver tongs for removing sugar cubes from sugar bowls, plump armchairs" (*G*, 162).

Metcalf's concern with the phonetic materiality of language and the plurality of signifieds generated by a signifier almost on that phonetic basis alone is everywhere evident in the story. The "repetitions and such words as 'padded' and 'plump' " in the above description "suggest a stifling comfort and, from David's point of view, a stultifying pointlessness" (BC, 176). In a later description of the surroundings of the Jubilee Street house, a description which functions both as an anticipation of what is to come once David is inside the house and as a metonymic index of Mrs. Heaney, the landlady, Metcalf draws attention in his commentary to the deliberate "harshness of five stresses in a row" in the clause "rusted iron stumps stuck up" (G, 163) and to the intentional "awkwardness" of the clause ". . . a small brown dog bunched, jerking tail . . ." (G, 163) created by "the unnatural placing of 'jerking' " (BC, 176).

Metcalf also speaks of the "hints of rhyme and near repetitions of sounds" in the phrase "the playing fields for employees" (G, 161), one of the details David sees from the train window, that are "suggestive of the confines from which David is escaping" (BC, 177) and of how the anticlimactic rhythm of the very first sentence of the story conveys emotion by building, through "delay, to no point at all, to *standing*, to silence" (BC, 177): "After David had again wrested the heavy suitcase from his father's obstinately polite grip and after he'd bought the ticket and assured his mother he wouldn't lose it, the three of them stood in the echoing booking hall of the railway station" (G, 159). The deflation here is paralleled on the train by the irony of his thinking the name of the street "Jubilee" "propitious" (G, 161) and by the deterioration of the "special," "regal," and "expansive" (G, 160) feeling he has once the mother and toddler join his carriage.

The most telling indication of the consciousness of the graphematic materiality of language, of how the signified slips incessantly under the signifier, of just how arbitrary the conventional relationship between signifier and signified is, of the infinite play of difference by which a word sends us off to other words instead of linking us directly with a world, is Jeremy's seemingly facetious discussion of words: "Don't you find that certain words make you think of things they don't mean? 'Emolument,' for example. Makes me think of very naked, very fat, black women. Something I read as a stripling about an African king's wives who were kept in pens and fed starchy tubers—so fat they couldn't get up—just rolled around—and *oiled* all over, rather like . . .' his hands sketched a shape '. . . rather like immense *seals* . . .' " (G, 171). Jeremy would no doubt agree with Roland Barthes when he says, "the signifier belongs to everybody,"[5] and when language is so openly displayed as a system of difference that allows for the production of multiple meanings, it undermines the idea of words as determinant signs.

That the eccentric character of Jeremy "is created almost entirely through dialogue and silences" (*BC*, 177) is no surprise, for it is a foregrounded method of characterization in Metcalf's fiction. Jeremy is a fictional descendant of Sebastian and his teddy-bear in Waugh's *Brideshead Revisited*, an ancestry suggested among other details by Jeremy's wish to be read a bedtime passage from Grahame's *The Wind in the Willows*. "Toad himself," Metcalf says, "suggests Jeremy's rather naughty inventiveness" and also "something of the spirit that David wishes for in his own life" (*BC*, 177). David's liberation through Jeremy is implied by his identification with Toad's epiphany in the passage he is reading and in the virtual report of a ship's departure in the final paragraph which signals closure: " '*All those wasted years,*' David continued reading aloud in the pink bedroom, '*that lie behind me, I never knew, never even* dreamt! *But* now—*but now that I know, now that I fully realize! Oh what a flowery track lies spread before me, henceforth! What dust-clouds shall spring up behind me as I speed on my reckless way!*' . . . Somewhere far distant in the night, in the docks perhaps, perhaps slipping its moorings and preparing to move out down the river to the sea, a ship was sounding and sounding" (*G*, 174). In answer to Jeremy's earlier question, "Are you the sort of person who lives in a place like this?" (*G*, 172) David finds that he is not the sort of person who would live at Mrs. Heaney's.

As the style of Jeremy's speech primarily indexes his character, not just its content, so too does the style of speech reveal the "demented garrulousness" of the "batty old man" (*BC*, 176), one of the inmates at the Jubilee house. He is one of those gathered for the "cooked evening meal," the description of which is an "extended exercise" (*BC*, 177) in metonymic setting and caricature. The bottle of cream soda stands for, is metonymically equivalent to, Mrs. Heaney, and "the ghastly array of sauce bottles," like the "garish plastic elephant" in David's room that Jeremy hurls into the night, "is 'shorthand' for a much longer description of this Hogarthian crew" (*BC*, 177): "In the centre of the oilcloth stood Heinz Ketchup, Cross and Blackwell's Salad Cream, HP Sauce, Branston Pickle, OK Sauce, Daddy's Favourite, A1 Sauce, a bottle of Camp Coffee, and a punctured tin of Nestlé's Evaporated Milk" (*G*, 166).

Finally, the story, as we have already seen, manifests Metcalf's principle of particularity everywhere: the "Balkan Sobranie cigarettes"; "the shape and weight of the wallet in his jacket's inside pocket. Stamped in gold inside the wallet were words that gave him obscure pleasure"; "the Cypriot barmaid whose upper front teeth were edged in gold" (G, 160); and "the backs of old jerrybuilt houses, cobbled streets, cemeteries, mouldering buildings housing strange companies found in the hidden ports of towns visible only from trains: *Victoria Sanitation and Brass, Global Furniture and Rattan, Allied Refuse*. Clothes lines. The narrow garden strips behind the houses looking as if receding waters had left there a tideline of haphazard junk" (G, 161)—all these and many more in addition to those noted earlier convey a concreteness. The story is, in short, one of Metcalf's finest.

Like "The Teeth of My Father" and *Private Parts,* another of Metcalf's finest stories "The Eastmill Reception Centre" is what Barthes would have called a "limit-text"—that is, a text that uses the conventions and modes of classic realism in such a way as to transgress classic realism itself. On the surface, this is a straightforward first-person narrative about a young university Education graduate's first teaching job at a state institution for male juvenile delinquents, but because of the materiality of all language, classic realism can never be secure. There are, for example, several fissures that disturb the surface of the text even before the main rupture that occurs two-thirds of the way through when the fictional, enunciating "I" steps forward and begins, "Well even that, I suppose, could do as an ending."[6] Consider, for example, the eight discontinuous narrative gaps that occur in the text up to this point where no narrative transitions are provided (E, 62, twice on 63, 64, twice on 67, 69, 70). These perforations fragment the fixed reality of the enounced that constitutes the story and the "I" speaking in the enounced, bearing witness to the text's activity of repression, as we so forcefully see after the main rupture that allows for the speaking of the Other: repressed desire.

Consider, too, the foregrounding of the materiality of language in relation to Dennis, one of the inmates, who is for the narrator, because of his repressed Lacanian desire, a displaced self, Dennis who because he doesn't "do writing" remains a decentered, uncentered self, unfixed in the Lacanian Symbolic order, that stabilizing

network of discourse and social formation that gives us our imaginary
identity:

> If I wrote *CAT*, he would stare at the word with a troubled frown. When
> I sounded out C-A-T, he would say indignantly: Well it's *cat*, isn't it?
> We had a cat, old tom cat. Furry knackers, he had, and if you stroked
> 'em . . .
> F-I-S-H brought to mind the chip shop up his street and his mum who
> wouldn't never touch rock salmon because it wasn't nothing but a fancy
> name for conger-eel.
> C-O-W evoked his Auntie Fran—right old scrubber *she* was, having it
> away for the price of a pint . . ."(*E,* 69).

These instances of arbitrary signification are complemented by the
later play on "bowel" and "vowel" and the multiple signifieds generated by "bail."

But although the Symbolic order, like the realist text, imposes
a shape on our needs, those needs—as the narrator who speaks from
the Other after the rupture of the text, apostrophizing the "absent"
Dennis, realizes—turns into desire: "You can't even begin to grasp
how appalling it is for me to say this. Say what? That my life,
respectable, sober, industrious, and civilized, above all civilized,
has at its core a desolating emptiness" (*E,* 75). This awareness of his
lack and incompleteness allows the narrator, in psychoanalytic terms,
to come into full contact with the primary language of desire, a
contact which does not yield stability, however, but an acceptance
that one's destiny as a subject is one of indefinite displacement and
that all language is the metonymic displacement of desire. He has
been led to this acceptance by his realization of the strange joy he
experienced in his vision of the town dump on fire, an occurrence
that disrupts his writing of the story and identifies him with Dennis
who also took a libidinous delight in fires.

The narrator has until this rupturing moment repressed these
elements of his psychic life that do not conform to the position he
has been assigned in the Symbolic order. For Lacan, as we saw in
our discussion of *Private Parts,* the play between presence and absence
that is essential to the functioning of language constitutes us as
desiring beings, for as a necessary condition of our speech, the "rest"
of language must be barred. As Colin MacCabe puts it, "And this
missing thing is not an unimportant theoretical postulate but the
necessarily recurrent question of our being. The process of loss which

enables us to gain language produces for us a place and an identity (a name and its substitution rules) within language, but this place is produced by the necessary absence of the differences that constitute it. . . . The unconscious is the result of the fact that, as we speak, what we say always escapes us—that as I (the ego) say one thing, it (the id) says something else."[7]

This lack overlaps another earlier lack in Lacanian theory "situated at the advent of the living being, that is to say, at sexed reproduction."[8] "By being subject to sex," an individual falls "under the blow of individual death," "loses that part of himself *qua* living being, in reproducing himself through the way of sex."[9] The narrator also faces this lack in his apostrophe to Dennis: "You don't understand, do you, what it means for me to make these confessions? To *have* to make these confessions, to face the death I feel inside myself?" (*E*, 75). But what is most interesting is that Lacan posits the myth of the lamella as the embodiment of the missing part constituted in the awareness of death, a myth which "designates the libido not as a field of forces, but as an organ."[10] He goes on to say:

This organ is unreal. Unreal is not imaginary. The unreal is defined by articulating itself on the real in a way that eludes us, and it is precisely this that requires that its representation should be mythical, as I have made it. But the fact that it is unreal does not prevent an organ from embodying itself. . . . One of the most ancient forms in which the unreal organ is incarnated in the body, is tattooing, scarification. The tattoo certainly has the function of being for the other, of situating the subject in it, marking his place in the field of the group's relations, between each individual and all the others. And, at the same time, it obviously has an erotic function. . . .[11]

Now we have heard Uncle Arthur warn the narrator early in the story to be on the lookout "for any lad as had a tattoo . . . because sure as the sun shines you've got trouble on your hands . . . most particularly . . . if it says, 'Mother' " (*E*, 62). Later in the story we see the tattoo of Dennis's friend, Paul, "a tattoo of a dagger on his left wrist and a red and green hummingbird on his right shoulder" (*E*, 69). Finally, after Dennis has been recaptured and severely punished, he asks to see the narrator, now teaching at another nearby school after having been dismissed for allowing the boys in his charge to escape. He's in the Eastmill Sick Bay: "He was obviously in pain, his face gaunt, the eyes big, but he smiled to see me and undid his pyjama jacket, carefully, slowly, lifting it aside to show me his chest. His brother, the one in the army who'd been home on leave, had paid for it. It was just possible to distinguish the outlines of a sailing ship through the crust of red and blue and green, the whole mess raised, heaving, cracking in furry scab" (*E*, 74). This is how the story ends, with the narrator wishing to situate himself as subject in the Other, to allow the unreal organ of the missing part to incarnate itself in the body:

> Let me try to put this in a different way. Let me try to find words that perhaps you'll understand. Words! Understand! Good Christ, will it never end, this blathering!
> Dennis. Dennis. Listen!
> Dennis, I envy you your—
> *Christ, man! Out with it!*
> Dennis. Listen to me.
> Concentrate.
> Dennis, I wish *I* had a tattoo. (*E*, 75–76)

The "blathering" here is the "talking cure" of psychoanalysis which he has undergone on his own in his address to the other, the displaced self embodied in Dennis, that allows for the speaking of the Other of repressed desire. As MacCabe says, "Psychoanalysis does not understand the patient's language as representing his or her experience but investigates the position allowed to the subject within his or her discourse. The process of the cure is the process by which new discourses open up fresh positions."[12] This is exactly what the discourse after the rupture does. Here the narrator seems to realize, in agreement with Lacan, that the person who speaks and is satisfied with what he says is not merely misguided but also wrong. Every statement that does not provoke change and uncentering within itself is wrong.

Our reading of "The Eastmill Reception Centre" has thus invoked analogies from psychoanalysis to explain not the workings of Metcalf's, the reader's, or even the central character's mind, but the workings of the text as a structure of desire. All of Metcalf's best texts are such structures.

# Chapter Eight
# Conclusion

If for Metcalf a story is "about" anything, it is "about the operation of language" (*KAP*, 22). In his short stories "it is language which speaks, not the author";[1] for language, because of its material laws, is always beyond the reach of conscious intention: "Sometimes writers do *not* know what a story is 'about'; the language itself reveals to them new directions, new dimensions as it unfolds. This is true for all writers to some degree or another; language is alive under their hands as clay is for a potter. Sometimes it has its own shape and insistence."[2]

We have seen this insistent materiality of language everywhere in Metcalf's texts when the signifier takes precedence over the signified: the foregrounding of speech as a narrative mode and the phonetic properties of signifiers in patterns of repetition, rhymes, and the rhythm of clauses and phrases; the possibilities of patterns of equivalence in the metaphoric and metonymic possibilities of language; and the slipping of the enounced away from the fictional enunciation. In Metcalf's best stories the language is indeed "alive," taking its own shape, but the two novels, especially *General Ludd,* attempt to ground language not in the signifier but in the signified. Because their overall design is ideological or thematic, they draw Metcalf away from the materialistic notion of language toward a notion of language as— especially paradoxical in the case of *General Ludd*—communication or expression. It is not language that speaks in *Going Down Slow* and *General Ludd,* but the "author." There is little room in the novels for readers.

But because the short stories and novellas are a polysemous space where the producer and reader of the text meet, *"in the text* only the reader speaks."[3] We write the texts we read, as Barthes says, in the sense that, because "the signifier belongs to everybody,"[4] we produce the meaning. Discourse is determined, in other words, both linguistically and subjectively. (It is also determined ideologically, for no text is innocent.) Because "no language has an edge over any other,"[5] however, because, as Lacan has taught us, there is no metalanguage, that producing of meaning, that speaking, that writing in the form of a critical discourse cannot be undertaken as if the critic is external to the language he is describing without smugness; for he or she is also in language. Consequently, the illusion of a metalanguage and the tone of smugness are most prominent in this study in the chapter on the novels, texts which beg for a critical metalanguage because of their own illusory ground of language.

In an attempt to mitigate this effect of the commentary as metalanguage, however, I have tried to display the texture of the fabric that is Metcalf's stories—for the text is etymologically a tissue, something woven, a fabric[6]—whenever possible and to examine Metcalf's various fictions in the narratological and rhetorical terms that view narrative as a fundamental system of intelligibility. Finally, in interpreting these texts I have tried to show that they are a flexible relationship of possibilities: both the possibilities of experience and the possibilities of language. Metcalf's best texts—and there are many of them—keep these possibilities forever open.

# Notes and References

*Preface*

    1. Kent Thompson, "John Metcalf: A Profile," *Fiddlehead*, no. 114 (Summer 1977), 63.

*Chapter One*

    1. For Saussure, on whose linguistic theory structuralism and post-structuralism are founded, the concept of language *(langue)* as merely a system of differences in which there are no positive terms is crucial. The sign (signifier plus signified) as a whole receives its meaning not by virtue of its reference to some object in the world, but by its specific differentiation from the entire body of other signs both in terms of signifiers and signifieds. A good introduction to Saussure is Jonathan Culler's book in the Modern Masters series, *Ferdinand de Saussure* (Glasgow: Fontana, 1976).

    2. See "Author's Commentary," in *Sixteen by Twelve: Short Stories by Canadian Writers,* ed. John Metcalf (Toronto: Ryerson Press, 1970), 198–203; hereafter cited as "Author's Commentary."

    3. Peter Brooks, "Fictions of the Wolfman," *Diacritics* 9 (Spring 1979):78.

    4. See James Guetti, "Theory Troubles," *Raritan* 3 (Spring 1984):130.

    5. All the biographical details related here have their source in Kent Thompson, "John Metcalf: A Profile," the letter Metcalf wrote Thompson on which the profile is based, or Douglas Rollins, "John Metcalf," in *Canadian Writers and Their Work,* vol. 7 (Downsview, Ont.: ECW Press, 1985), 155–58.

    6. Quoted by Thompson, in "Profile," 58.

    7. Letter to Kent Thompson, Spring 1977.

    8. Quoted by Thompson, in "Profile," 59.

    9. Ibid., 58.

    10. Letter to Kent Thompson, Spring 1977.

    11. Ibid.

    12. Douglas Rollins, "The Montreal Storytellers," *Journal of Canadian Fiction* 1 (Spring 1972):5.

    13. Ibid.

    14. Geoff Hancock, "Communique: *Interview with John Metcalf—* February 16, 1981," in *Kicking Against the Pricks* (Downsview, Ont.: ECW Press, 1982), 14.

15. Reingard M. Nischik, "John Metcalf et al. Make It New: The Short Story in Canada," paper delivered at the Conference for *Gesellschaft Fur Kanada-Studien,* March 1984.

16. "The Curate's Egg," *Essays in Canadian Writing,* no. 30 (Winter 1984–85), 52.

17. Gérard Genette, *Narrative Discourse: An Essay in Method,* trans. Jane E. Lewin (Ithaca: Cornell University Press, 1980), 163–64.

18. Barry Cameron, "The Practice of the Craft: A Conversation with John Metcalf," *Queen's Quarterly* 82 (Autumn 1975):416. See Roland Barthes, *Le Grain de la voix Entretiens 1962–1980* (Paris: Seuil, 1981), 184.

19. "Building Castles," in *Making It New: Contemporary Canadian Stories* (Toronto: Methuen, 1982), 179.

20. "Author's Commentary," 202.

21. "Building Castles," 179–80. For an extended discussion of the notion of game and play in literature, see Peter Hutchinson, *Games Authors Play* (London: Methuen, 1983).

22. "The Curate's Egg," 52.

23. Hancock, "Communique," 17.

24. John Metcalf, ed., *New Worlds: A Canadian Collection of Stories with Notes* (Toronto: McGraw-Hill Ryerson, 1980), 163.

25. Ibid., 7.

26. See "The Curate's Egg," 54, and Cameron, "The Practice of the Craft," 402. Foregrounding does not imply a single linguistic norm, for what is "automatized" in one kind of discourse will become foregrounded when transferred to another. That which is foregrounded, too, is always in dialectic with a "background": so-called ordinary language, literary tradition, and the linguistic norms established by the text itself. See David Lodge, *The Modes of Modern Writing: Metaphor, Metonym, and the Typology of Modern Literature* (London: Edward Arnold, 1979), 23; originally published in 1977. The 1979 edition contains an important "Prefatory Note to the Second Impression." Because it is so prevalent, metonymy is crucial to understanding how fiction works. It is a figure that names an attribute, adjunct, cause, or effect of the thing instead of the thing itself. Another important figure for fiction related to metonymy is synecdoche, a figure that names a part for the whole, the whole for a part, the species for the genus, the genus for the species, or the name of the material for the thing made. Both figures are commonplace devices in our ordinary speech.

27. "The Curate's Egg," 54, and "Building Castles," 177.

28. Hancock, "Communique," 5.

29. Ibid., 6.

30. Letter received from John Metcalf, 31 May 1980.

31. "Building Castles," 175.

32. Ibid.

33. Letter received from John Metcalf, 8 June 1980.
34. *New Worlds,* 147.
35. Ibid., 149.
36. Jerome Beaty, *The Norton Introduction to Fiction,* 2d ed. (New York: W. W. Norton, 1981), 56.

*Chapter Two*

1. "Author's Commentary," 202.
2. A useful way to understand scenic report is to think of it, by way of analogy to film, as a visual synecdoche, a close-up of action. See Helmut Bonheim, *The Narrative Modes: Techniques of the Short Story* (Cambridge, England: D. S. Brewer, 1982) for useful discussions of the four primary narrative modes, conventions of beginning and ending (closure), and the importance of understanding rhetorical figures for an analysis of fiction.
3. "Every title . . . has several simultaneous meanings, including at least these two: (i) what it says linked to the contingency of what follows it; (ii) the announcement itself that a piece of literature (which means, in fact, a commodity) is going to follow" (Roland Barthes, "Textual Analysis of Poe's Valdemar," in *Untying the Text: A Post-Structuralist Reader,* ed. Robert Young [London: Routledge & Kegan Paul, 1981], 139).
4. In *Modern Canadian Stories,* ed. Giose Rimanelli and Roberto Ruberto (Toronto: McGraw-Hill Ryerson, 1966).
5. This desire of the repressed, the Other, to speak is, as we shall see, the axis of one of Metcalf's recent stories, "The Eastmill Reception Centre."
6. Is this "nightmare babble of voices" in the staff room the equivalent of Eliot's recurring lines, "In the room the women come and go / Talking of Michelangelo"?
7. See Shlomith Rimmon-Kenan, *Narrative Fiction: Contemporary Poetics* (London: Methuen, 1983), 48.
8. See Roland Barthes, "Introduction to the Structural Analysis of Narratives," in *Image—Music—Text* (New York: Hill and Wang, 1977), 93–94; and Seymour Chatman, *Story and Discourse: Narrative Structure in Fiction and Film* (Ithaca: Cornell University Press, 1978), 53–56.
9. See Roger Sale, "Introduction," *The Wind in the Willows* (New York: Bantam, 1982), x.
10. Rollins, "John Metcalf," 172.
11. A "small film" is "a low-budget black-and-white film shot in the Academy frame format with television techniques and concerned with the everyday lives of ordinary people," David A. Cook, *A History of Narrative Film* (New York: W. W. Norton, 1981), 440. The story appeared

in *Edge*, no. 6 (Spring 1967), 19–24; the two quotations are from pages 23 and 24 respectively.

    12. *KAP*, 105.

    13. "Playground," *Queen's Quarterly* 85 (Spring 1978):28.

    14. Metcalf comments on his use of italics in this process in his discussion of a passage that occurs early in the story when the character-focalizer picks up his daughter at her maternal grandmother's. See *KAP*, 106. For a discussion of types of speech representation in fiction, see Rimmon-Kenan, *Narrative Fiction*, 106–16.

    15. Cameron, "The Practice of the Craft," 421.

    16. Ibid.

    17. Chatman, *Story and Discourse*, 48.

    18. "Author's Commentary," 202.

*Chapter Three*

    1. "Author's Commentary," 199.

    2. Jerome Beaty, *Norton Introduction to Fiction*, 163.

    3. "Author's Commentary," 201; Hancock, "Communique," 22; and Cameron, "The Practice of the Craft," 422.

    4. Genette in his discussion of the temporal component, frequency, in narrative distinguishes among three basic repetition-relations between story events and their narration: singulative, telling once what happened once and, less frequently, telling *x* times what happened *x* times; repetitive, telling *x* times what happened once; and iterative, telling once what happened *x* times. See his *Narrative Discourse*, 113–60.

    5. See *KAP*, 39, and Cameron, "The Practice of the Craft," 411.

    6. The use of the figures of repetition—anadiplosis (repetition of the last word of one clause to begin the next), anaphora (repetition of the same word at the beginning of successive clauses), and polysyndeton (the repetition of conjunctions)—masculine rhyme, and sentence fragments is particularly effective in a passage that leads up to their release here: "And then they were running. Running with their mouths open and their hearts pounding; running and stumbling for dear life through the heavy sand of the dunes. They did not look back, but ran and ran until the blood pounded in their temples and their throats were dry and aching and they could run no more. Eventually, with shaking legs, they collapsed into the dunes near their favourite cliff" (*NCW*, 6).

    7. William Golding's *Lord of the Flies*, another story concerned with the fall of children, is intertextually relevant.

    8. We shall see a tattoo on another lad from Borstal in "The Eastmill Reception Centre."

    9. "I've Got It Made," *Canadian Forum*, April 1965, 13.

10. "A Bag of Cherries," in *Sixteen by Twelve,* 180; hereafter cited in the text as *ST* with page number.

11. "Author's Commentary," 200.

12. Ibid. What does the absence of these cartridge cases among the inventory of stored items from his childhood in the attic (182) imply? Has Metcalf missed an opportunity to amplify the metonymic significance of the cases?

*Chapter Four*

1. Robert Scholes, *Semiotics and Interpretation* (New Haven: Yale University Press, 1982), 117.

2. See Chatman, *Story and Discourse,* 33–34.

3. Compare Metcalf's use of the same strategy in "Walking Around the City" in which the horror of the indifference of the world to the plight of the wounded dog exceeds the horror of the dog's condition.

4. He limits his alcoholic consumption, for example, and retires to bed at a reasonable hour. He gives himself plenty of time to prepare for his performance, and he is concerned about the possibility of one of his fellow actors, Pasmore, flubbing his lines because he has been drinking in the afternoon.

5. In "Building Castles," 178–79, Metcalf comments on the caricature of Charles Pevency, the book review editor in the story, on the materiality of language, and on the metonymic significations in the description of the suburban house to which Haine goes to read his poems only because he needs money and wishes to eat.

6. Notice that Haine has stuffed the doorbell with paper, an item identified with his craft, writing. In "Punctuation as Score," in *KAP,* 98–100, Metcalf comments on this whole opening passage in terms of the materiality of language again. He remarks on his use of single quotation marks where double would be expected to suggest distance, on his use of italics to render interior speech, and on his use of double quotation marks to contribute "to action and to our awareness of Haine's consciousness" (100).

7. See Italo Calvino, "Notes towards a definition of the narrative form as a combinative process," *Twentieth Century Studies* 3 (May 1970):96.

8. See Catherine Belsey, *Critical Practice* (London: Methuen, 1980), 85–102.

*Chapter Five*

1. E. D. Blodgett, "Forming Other Connections: Ethel Wilson's Novellas," *Canadian Storyteller* (forthcoming).

2. Jerome Beaty, *The Norton Introduction to the Shorter Novel* (New York: W. W. Norton, 1982), xi–xvi.

3. Mary Doyle Springer, *Forms of the Modern Novella* (Chicago: University of Chicago Press, 1975), 102.

4. Metcalf's finals essay, "The Creative Imagination," explored the notions of creative and conservative man and woman in Cary's fiction.

5. In "The Geography of Time: Part One," *Prism International* 4, no. 1 (Summer 1964).

6. Compare Metcalf's remarks in "Author's Commentary," where he speaks of everyone in our lives as a sort of hypotyposis: "Perhaps we invent everyone we know? Perhaps we simplify them and shape them to fit our needs? Perhaps we invent ourselves?" (201).

7. Compare Charles Ryder's tendency in Waugh's *Brideshead Revisited* to see Julia's guilt as drama or a pre-Raphaelite painting.

8. In "Punctuation as Score," in *KAP*, 105, Metcalf writes of his reasons for using italics in the passages with Trevore, of Trevore as an example of economic caricature, and of the ashtray as a metonym of Trevore.

9. Metcalf discusses the orchestration of dialogue and the "way in which speech can be punctuated" by means of nondialogued paragraphed lines in the sections that concern Elspeth McCleod (*KAP*, 11–12).

10. G. C. Argan, *The Renaissance*, vol. 3 of *The Dolphin History of Painting* (London: Thames & Hudson, 1969), 138.

11. All of these reflective instances produce the effect of an enunciating "I" that is aware of the division between enounced and enunciation, signified and signifier, but this "I" is really just another external narrator. The real enunciating "I" is either Metcalf the scriptor during the process of producing the text through writing or the reader during the process of reading.

12. See Belsey, *Critical Practice*, 85–102.

13. Jacques Lacan's writing is extremely difficult, and while the explanation offered here is simplified, I hope it is not distorted. I am much indebted to Malcolm Bowie's essay on Lacan in *Structuralism and Since: From Levi-Strauss to Derrida*, ed. John Sturrock (Oxford: Oxford University Press, 1979), 116–53; Anthony Wilden's surrounding commentary on Lacan's "The Function of Language in Psychoanalysis" in *Speech and Language in Psychoanalysis* (Baltimore: Johns Hopkins University Press, 1981); and Antony Easthope's discussion of Lacan in *Poetry as Discourse* (London: Methuen, 1983), 30–47. Some of Lacan's seminars are available in translation in *Écrits: A Selection,* trans. Alan Sheridan (New York: W. W. Norton, 1977) and *The Four Fundamental Concepts of Psycho-Analysis* (New York: W. W. Norton, 1978).

14. The child can only begin to use language in a coherent way by "subjecting" itself to the Symbolic order, taking up a position in this system of conventions. The child must identify itself with certain terms— "girl," "boy," "daughter," "son"—terms which receive their significance by their relation to a central signifier, the Phallus, the signifier of desire and of a potential power in its possessor, the Paternal Law, the "Father." The child can only resolve the threat of castration and the Oedipal complex by submitting to this paternal authority and simultaneously identifying with it. The child is thus assigned a position in language, in the family, and in sexuality. The repression of those elements of the psychic life that do not conform to this positioning constitutes the unconscious, which, because it is structured like a language, is the discourse of the Other ("lack," "gap," "absence"). The subject is constantly troubled by the return of the repressed: verbal slips, hysterical symptoms, dreams.

15. Desire is insatiable because it is desire of a Symbolic position— the position that is powerful, self-constituting, the source of the law, the arbiter of the possibilities of the expression of desire—not of a real person. The desired object, like the disseminated signified, constantly recedes.

16. "Notes on Writing a Story," *Fiddlehead*, no. 114 (Summer 1977):68; hereafter cited in the text as *N* with page number.

17. Michael Westlake, *One Zero and the Night Controller*. Quoted by Anthony Easthope, *Poetry as Discourse*, 3.

18. Desire involves the constant displacement of energy from object to object and is thus, for Lacan, metonymic. The narrator's journey through various displaced art forms is a structure of desire, and all the art forms are metonyms of "Bobby's thing," the Phallus, the wielder of power.

19. At first glance, these metanarrative moments seem to be no more than a traditional, not a post-Saussurean, antirealist position that no language, no discourse, can ever be adequate to the multifarious nature of the real, a position, as Colin MacCabe points out, that still "assumes the classic realist division of language and reality" (*James Joyce and the Revolution of the Word* [London: Macmillan Press, 1978], 15). But they are also manifestations of the desire of the Other to speak and of Lacan's notion of the Real, that upon which language is at work, that which lies beyond the insistence of the linguistic sign. The Real, however, should not be confused with reality.

20. In another context, Robert Scholes (*Fabulation and Metafiction* [Urbana: University of Illinois Press, 1979], 12) has this to say about the displacements and misrecognitions in mirrors: "Mirrors . . . are superbly iconic in their reflections of reality, but patently artificial in at least three

respects. They reduce three dimensions to a plane surface of two, they double distance and reduce size (our face in a mirror is only half its true size), and . . . they reverse right and left."

*Chapter Six*

1. Max Stirner's principal writings are *The Ego and One's Own*, 1845, and *The History of the Reaction*, 2 vols., 1852. See George Woodcock, *Anarchism: A History of Libertarian Ideas and Movements* (1962; reprint, Harmondsworth: Penguin, 1975), and his essay, "on Being Inadmissible," *New York Review of Books*, 27 September 1984, 42–44.

2. John Metcalf, Letter to Douglas Rollins, May 1966.

3. Metcalf is aware of these possible liabilities, as his remarks in an interview suggest when he speaks of the external pressures involved to produce a first novel. See Cameron, "The Practice of the Craft," 403–14. The title of the novel, as Rollins notes in "John Metcalf," 182, derives from a blues song of the same name by St. Louis Jimmy Oden: "I have had my fun; if I don't get well no more, / My health is failing me, and I'm going down slow."

4. It first appeared on the weekly CBC broadcast, *Anthology*.

5. In his discussion of Waugh's relationship to stage farce and the Commedia dell' Arte, Martin Green notes that one of the central trio of characters in the Commedia, Pierrot (the others are Harlequin and Colombine), yearns for beauty in general and that Jules Laforgue identified himself as poet with Pierrot: "He gave the figure its modern reference to the artist isolated among crudely normal Philistines, [and] its modern setting, the waste-land townscape . . ." [*Transatlantic Patterns: Cultural Comparisons of England with America* (New York: Basic Books, 1977), 92].

6. Susan Rubin Suleiman, *Authoritarian Fictions: The Ideological Novel as a Literary Genre* (New York: Columbia University Press, 1983), 1.

7. Hancock, "Communique," 27.

8. W. H. New, "The Flowers that Bloom in L.A." [Editorial], *Canadian Literature*, no. 98 (Autumn 1983), 3.

9. Hancock, "Communique," 27.

10. A remark once made by James Wolcott.

11. An ideological analogue to Henry Benson is John Gardner in *Going Down Slow*.

12. David Lodge, "Evelyn Waugh: Habits of a Lifetime," in *Working with Structuralism: Essays and Reviews on Nineteenth- and Twentieth-Century Literature* (London: Routledge & Kegan Paul, 1981), 123.

13. Ibid., 123–24.

14. Hancock, "Communique," 27.

15. Belsey, *Critical Practice*, 4.

16. Ibid.
17. Ibid., 7.
18. Green, *Transatlantic Patterns*, 82.

*Chapter Seven*

1. Christopher Lasch, "The Great American Variety Show," *New York Review of Books*, 2 February 1984, 36, col. 4.
2. In *Making It New*.
3. "Building Castles," 175; hereafter cited in the text as *BC* followed by page number.
4. "Single Gents Only," in *Making It New: Contemporary Canadian Stories* (Toronto: Methuen, 1982), 159; hereafter cited in the text as *G* followed by page number.
5. Barthes, "Theory of the Text," in *Untying the Text*, 37.
6. "The Eastmill Reception Centre," *Fiddlehead*, no. 14 (Winter 1981), 72; hereafter cited in the text as *E* followed by page number.
7. MacCabe, *James Joyce and the Revolution of the Word*, 7.
8. Jacques Lacan, "The Subject and Other: Alienation" in *The Four Fundamental Concepts of Psycho-Analysis*, 205.
9. Ibid.
10. Ibid.
11. Ibid., 205–6.
12. MacCabe, *James Joyce and the Revolution of the Word*, 8.

*Chapter Eight*

1. Roland Barthes, "The Death of the Author," in *Image—Music—Text*, 143.
2. "The Curate's Egg," 50–51.
3. Roland Barthes, *S/Z*, trans. Richard Miller (London: Cape, 1975), 151.
4. Barthes, "Theory of the Text," 37.
5. Ibid., 43.
6. Ibid., 39.

# Selected Bibliography

All of Metcalf's most important publications are listed chronologically under primary sources subdivided into Fiction, Nonfiction, and Works Edited. Only selected items are listed under secondary sources.

## PRIMARY SOURCES

### 1. Fiction

"The Geography of Time: Part One." *Prism International* 4, no. 1 (Summer 1964):7–30.

"The Geography of Time: Part Two." *Prism International* 4, no. 2 (Autumn 1964):29–43.

"I've Got It Made." *Canadian Forum,* April 1965, 12–13.

"One for Cupid." *Edge,* no. 6 (Spring 1967):19–24.

*New Canadian Writing, 1969: Stories by John Metcalf, D. O. Spittique and C. J. Newman.* Toronto: Clarke, Irwin, 1969.

"A Bag of Cherries." In *Sixteen by Twelve,* edited by John Metcalf, 180–85. Toronto: Ryerson Press, 1970.

*The Lady Who Sold Furniture.* Toronto: Clarke, Irwin, 1970.

*Going Down Slow.* Toronto: McClelland & Stewart, 1972. Reprint. Don Mills, Ont.: PaperJacks, 1975.

*The Teeth of My Father.* Ottawa: Oberon, 1975.

Metcalf, John, and John Newlove. *Dreams Surround Us: Fiction and Poetry.* Delta, Ont.: Bastard, 1977.

"Playground." *Queen's Quarterly* 85 (1978):17–31.

*Girl in Gingham.* Ottawa: Oberon, 1978.

*Private Parts: A Memoir.* Scarborough, Ont.: New American Library, 1980.

*General Ludd.* Downsview, Ont.: ECW, 1980. Reprint. Don Mills, Ont.: General Paperbacks, 1981.

"The Eastmill Reception Centre." *Fiddlehead,* no. 128 (Winter 1981): 59–76.

"Single Gents Only." In *Making It New: Contemporary Canadian Stories.* Edited by John Metcalf. Toronto: Methuen, 1982.

*Selected Stories.* New Canadian Library, no. 168. Toronto: McClelland & Stewart, 1982.

"Travelling Northward." *Malahat Review: A Special Issue on John Metcalf,* no. 70 (March 1985): 17–71.

2. Nonfiction

"Notes on Writing a Story." *Fiddlehead,* no. 114 (Summer 1977):68–72.
*Kicking against the Pricks.* Downsview, Ont.: ECW, 1982.
"What Happened to Canlit?" *Globe and Mail,* Books Literary Supplement, 19 November 1983, 1.
"The Curate's Egg." *Essays on Canadian Writing,* no. 30 (Winter 1984–85):35–59.
"Paintings About Painting: Notes Towards an Essay on Tony Calzetta." *Malahat Review: A Special Issue on John Metcalf,* no. 70 (March 1985):81–97.

3. Works Edited

Metcalf, John, ed. *Sixteen by Twelve: Short Stories by Canadian Writers.* Toronto: Ryerson, 1970.
————. *The Narrative Voice: Short Stories and Reflections by Canadian Authors.* Toronto: McGraw-Hill Ryerson, 1972.
Blaise, Clark, and John Metcalf, eds. *Here & Now: Best Canadian Stories.* Ottawa: Oberon, 1977.
Metcalf, John, ed. *Stories Plus: Canadian Stories with Authors' Commentaries.* Toronto: McGraw-Hill Ryerson, 1979.
————. *New Worlds: A Canadian Collection of Stories with Notes.* Toronto: McGraw-Hill Ryerson, 1980.
————. *The Literary Review. On the Edge: Canadian Short Stories,* 28 (Spring 1985).

SECONDARY SOURCES

Cameron, Barry. "The Practice of the Craft: A Conversation with John Metcalf." *Queen's Quarterly* 82 (1975):402–24. An important interview that reveals Metcalf's concern with the materiality of language and rhetorical strategies.
————. "An Approximation of Poetry: The Short Stories of John Metcalf." *Studies in Canadian Literature* 2 (1977):17–35. A detailed study of the stories that concern artists and art.
————. "Invention in *Girl in Gingham.*"*Fiddlehead,* no. 114 (Summer 1977):57–63. A meticulous analysis of the metaphoric and metonymic significance of the details of the novella.
————. Review of *Kicking against the Pricks.* "Letters in Canada." *University of Toronto Quarterly* 52 (Summer 1983):482–85. Discusses the cultural/sociological importance of the book.

**Garebian, Keith.** " 'General Ludd': A Satire on Decadence." *Canadian Literature,* no. 101 (Summer 1984):43–55. "Metcalf uses fiction's mirrors like an expert, showing an age its own grimaces, japes, and follies with witty grace."

**Lecker, Robert.** *On the Line: Readings in the Short Fiction of Clark Blaise, John Metcalf, and Hugh Hood,* 59–97. Downsview, Ont.: ECW Press, 1982. Shows how *"ideas* develop through Metcalf's concentration on *things"* by tracing the evolution of Metcalf's aesthetic in the growth of his protagonist from boyhood to manhood.

**Rollins, Douglas.** "John Metcalf." *Canadian Writers and Their Work.* Fiction Series. Edited by Robert Lecker, Jack David, Ellen Quigley, 155–211. Downsview, Ont.: ECW Press, 1985. A good general introduction to Metcalf's fiction that contains an extensive bibliography of secondary sources.

**Rooke, Constance,** ed. *Malahat Review: A Special Issue on John Metcalf,* no. 70 (March 1985). Contains tributes by Alice Munro and Keith Fraser, essays on the novellas by Keith Garebian and Constance Rooke, an essay on *Ludd* by George Woodcock, and an important reading of "The Estuary" by Simone Vauthier in terms of narratology.

**Thompson, Kent.** "John Metcalf: A Profile." *Fiddlehead,* no. 114 (Summer 1977):57–63. Both a tribute and an important source of biographical information.

# Index

Amis, Kingsley, 10, 11
*amorce*, 23, 27
anadiplosis, 132n6
anaphora, 30, 50, 132n6
anarchism, 102–103, 110, 111
Argan, G. C., 87
Atwood, Margaret, 118
Auden, W. H., 115
autobiography and autobiographical, 14, 37, 73, 74–75, 92
auxesis, 22

"Bag of Cherries, A," 36, 47, 54–56
Barthes, Roland, 7, 24, 120, 122, 126
Beaty, Jerome, 13, 15, 36–37, 77
"Beef Curry, The," 15–17
Belsey, Catherine, 75, 92. *See also* interrogative text
"Beryl," 47, 50–54
*Best Canadian Stories*, 6
bildungsroman, 15, 92
biography, 1
Birney, Earle, 3
"Biscuits," 36, 37–38, 39
Blaise, Clark, 5
Brechtian alienation, 75
Brooks, Peter, 1

Calvino, Italo, 70
Canada Council, 4, 5
Cary, Joyce, 2–3, 92; creative and conservative individual in, 78 103, 134n4; *House of Children, A,* 43; *To Be a Pilgrim,* 71, 72

"Dandelions," 31–32
Davies Robertson, 118
disguised definition, 3

"Early Morning Rabbits," 3, 36, 40, 43
"Eastmill Reception Centre, The," 10, 23, 122–125
effaced narrator, 13
Eliot, T.S., 9, 27; "Love Song of J. Alfred Prufrock, The," 16, 22, 23
ellipsis, 10

enunciation and enounced, 70, 73, 92, 93, 96, 122, 126, 134n11
epanalepsis, 17, 19, 22, 31, 43, 44
epizeuxis, 41
"Estuary, The," 4, 32–35
existents, 32
expressive realism, 112–114. *See also* ideology of common sense

fabulation, 75
Falstaff, 79. *See also* Shakespeare
Faulkner, 115
fiction, as product of history and reader, 1, 8; nature of, 7, 71, 72, 73, 74, 76. *See also* reading
"Flowers that Bloom in the Spring," 103
focalization, 13, 59, *passim*
foregrounding, 10, 130n26
Forster, E. M., 11
Fraser, Ray, 5
Freud, 114
Frye, Northrop, 1

Gallant, Mavis, vii
*General Ludd,* 6, 10, 102, 103, 109–116, 126
Gennette, Gérard, 7, 23
genre, 77
"Gentle as Flowers Make the Stones," 8, 57, 66–70
"Geography of the House," 17–18
"Geography of Time, The," 15–26, 40
Giorgione: *Tempesta,* 87
*"Girl in Gingham,"* 5–6, 17, 23, 82–91
*Girl in Gingham,* 6
*Going Down Slow,* 4–5, 15, 102, 103–109, 110, 126
Grahame, Kenneth: *Wind in the Willows,* 25, 121

Hancock, Geoff, 6
"Happiest Days, The," 4, 18, 2–23
Hemingway, Ernest, 3, 17, 25; "Cat in the Rain," 25; "Hills Like White Elephants," 25
Hood, Hugh, 5

141